VIOLENCE IN FILM AND TELEVISION

Violence in Film and Television

JAMES D. TORR
Book Editor

Daniel Leone,
President

Bonnie Szumski,
Publisher

Scott Barbour,
Managing Editor

James D. Torr,
Series Editor

Greenhaven Press, Inc.
San Diego, California

Every effort has been made to trace the owners of copyrighted material. The articles in this volume may have been edited for content, length, and/or reading level. The titles have been changed to enhance the editorial purpose.

No part of this book may be reproduced or used in any form or by any means, electrical, mechanical, or otherwise, including, but not limited to, photocopy, recording, or any information storage and retrieval system, without prior written permission from the publisher.

Library of Congress Cataloging-in-Publication Data

Violence in film and television / James D. Torr, book editor.
p. cm.—(Examining pop culture)
Includes bibliographical references and index.
ISBN 0-7377-0864-6 (pbk. : alk. paper).—
ISBN 0-7377-0865-4 (lib. : alk. paper).—
1. Violence in motion pictures. 2. Violence on television.
I. Torr, James D., 1974–   II. Series.

PN1995.9.V5 V545   2002
303.6'0973—dc21   2001023915
                                                              CIP

Cover Photo: © Michael Grecco/Stock, Boston, Inc./Picture Quest

© 2002 by Greenhaven Press, Inc.
10911 Technology Place, San Diego, CA 92127

Printed in the U.S.A.

CONTENTS

Chapter 2: Violence on Television

Chapter 4: Debating Screen Violence: Artistic Value vs. Societal Harm

Chapter 5: Responding to Violence in Popular Entertainment

POPULAR CULTURE IS THE COMMON SET OF ARTS, entertainments, customs, beliefs, and values shared by large segments of society. Russel B. Nye, one of the founders of the study of popular culture, wrote that "not until the appearance of mass society in the eighteenth century could popular culture, as one now uses the term, be said to exist." According to Nye, the Industrial Revolution and the rise of democracy in the eighteenth and nineteenth centuries led to increased urbanization and the emergence of a powerful middle class. In nineteenth-century Europe and North America, these trends created audiences for the popular arts that were larger, more concentrated, and more well off than at any point in history. As a result, more people shared a common culture than ever before.

The technological advancements of the twentieth century vastly accelerated the spread of popular culture. With each new advance in mass communication—motion pictures, radio, television, and the Internet—popular culture has become an increasingly pervasive aspect of everyday life.

Popular entertainment—in the form of movies, television, theater, music recordings and concerts, books, magazines, sporting events, video games, restaurants, casinos, theme parks, and other attractions—is one very recognizable aspect of popular culture. In his 1999 book *The Entertainment Economy: How Mega-Media Forces Are Transforming Our Lives*, Michael J. Wolf argues that entertainment is becoming the dominant feature of American society: "In choosing where we buy French fries, how we relate to political candidates, what airline we want to fly, what pajamas we choose for our kids, and which mall we want to buy them in, entertainment is increasingly influencing every one of those choices. . . . Multiply that by the billions of choices that, collectively, all of us make each day and you have a portrait of a society in which entertainment is one of its leading institutions."

It is partly this pervasive quality of popular culture that makes it worthy of study. James Combs, the author of *Polpop: Politics and Popular Culture in America*, explains that examining popular culture is important because it can shape people's attitudes and beliefs:

> Popular culture is so much a part of our lives that we cannot deny its developmental powers. . . . Like formal education or family rearing, popular culture is part of our "learning environment.". . . Though our pop culture education is informal—we usually do not attend to pop culture for its "educational" value—it nevertheless provides us with information and images upon which we develop our opinions and attitudes. We would not be what we are, nor would our society be quite the same, without the impact of popular culture.

Examining popular culture is also important because popular movies, music, fads, and the like often reflect popular opinions and attitudes. Christopher D. Geist and Jack Nachbar explain in *The Popular Culture Reader*, "the popular arts provide a gauge by which we can learn what Americans are thinking, their fears, fantasies, dreams, and dominant mythologies. The popular arts reflect the values of the multitude."

This two-way relationship between popular culture and society is evident in many modern discussions of popular culture. Does the glorification of guns by many rap artists, for example, merely reflect the realities of inner-city life, or does it also contribute to the problem of gun violence? Such questions also arise in discussions of the popular culture of the past. Did the Vietnam protest music of the late 1960s and early 1970s, for instance, simply reflect popular antiwar sentiments, or did it help turn public opinion against the war? Examining such questions is an important part of understanding history.

Greenhaven Press's Examining Pop Culture series provides students with the resources to begin exploring these questions. Each volume in the series focuses on a particular aspect of popular culture, with topics as varied as popular culture itself. Books in the series may focus on a particular genre, such as *Rap and Hip Hop*, while others may cover a specific medium, such as *Computers and the Internet*. Volumes such as *Body Piercing and Tattoos* have their focus on recent trends in popular culture, while titles like *Americans' Views About War* have a broader historical scope.

In each volume, an introductory essay provides a general

overview of the topic. The selections that follow offer a survey of critical thought about the subject. The readings in *Americans' Views About War*, for example, are arranged chronologically: Essays explore how popular films, songs, television programs, and even comic books both reflected and shaped public opinion about American wars from World War I through Vietnam. The essays in *Violence in Film and Television*, on the other hand, take a more varied approach: Some provide historical background, while others examine specific genres of violent film, such as horror, and still others discuss the current controversy surrounding the issue.

Each book in the series contains a comprehensive index to help readers quickly locate material of interest. Perhaps most importantly, each volume has an annotated bibliography to aid interested students in conducting further research on the topic. In today's culture, what is "popular" changes rapidly from year to year and even month to month. Those who study popular culture must constantly struggle to keep up. The volumes in Greenhaven's Examining Pop Culture series are intended to introduce readers to the major themes and issues associated with each topic, so they can begin examining for themselves what impact popular culture has on their own lives.

WHEN IT COMES TO TELEVISION AND FILM VIO-
lence, according to Joseph Lieberman, a U.S. senator and the
2000 Democratic nominee for vice president, "the question
most Americans seem to be asking is not whether the roman-
ticized and sanitized vision of violence the entertainment media present to our kids is in fact harmful, but what we as a national family are going to do about it." Lieberman's sentiments
are echoed by many policy makers, parents, and critics who are
convinced that movie and television violence present a grave
threat to America's youth.

The Controversy

At a 1999 Senate hearing on media violence, Donald E. Cook,
president of the American Academy of Pediatrics, warned that
exposure to violent entertainment "results in increased acceptance of violence as an appropriate means of conflict resolution." In his book *Hollywood vs. America*, film critic Michael
Medved states that Hollywood "glorifies violence as an enjoyable adventure and manly ideal" and warns that "a wealth of
scientific studies" have "removed most of the remaining doubts
about the link between make believe brutality and real world
aggression." A 1999 issue of *American Enterprise* notes that
"more than seven out of ten Americans say they think the TV
industry needs to do more to reduce the amount of violence it
unleashes on the public."

The popularity of violent films and television series, however, indicates that a significant portion of Americans want violence in their entertainment. Moreover, screen violence has
its defenders. Some take issue with the research on media violence, pointing out that it is very difficult to prove why some
individuals tend toward violence while others do not. Others
worry that the government might censor movies and television
shows that feature violence. Jack Valenti, the president of the
Motion Picture Association of America, states that "in a free
society, no one can command 'only good movies be produced.'" Sociology professor Barry Glassner argues that the

controversy over media violence draws attention from the real problem of gun violence: "TV shows do not kill or maim people," he writes, "guns do." The *Nation's* Katha Pollitt maintains that violence in the media reflects the violence in society: "Violent and stupid entertainment is popular because it corresponds to reality, which is often violent and stupid."

An Ancient Tradition

Violent entertainment was popular long before movies and television existed. Famous examples of violent literature include the ancient Greek poet Homer's the *Iliad* and the *Odyssey*, which contain graphic depictions of bloodshed. The ancient Romans enjoyed watching gladiatorial combat. Many of Shakespeare's plays feature murder, suicide, and swordplay. *Punch and Judy*, a puppet show popular at fairs in Victorian England, opens with the character of Punch beating his dog and killing his wife. As *Journal of Popular Film & Television* editor Harvey Roy Greenberg notes, "Chronicles of aggression—spoken, sung, danced, written, drawn—have appeared in virtually every recorded clime and time."

The ancient tradition of violent entertainment seems to reflect the fact that violence is a dominant theme in history. "We are a violent species, and we were long before video games or any other form of electronic media could be blamed," writes Joan E. Bertin of the National Coalition Against Censorship. "Think of the Crusades, the Inquisition, the Holocaust and other institutionalized forms of torture and violence." James B. Twitchell, the author of *Preposterous Violence: Fables of Aggression in Modern Culture*, offers a more specific explanation for the popularity of violent entertainment. He believes that stories of violence, both ancient and modern, are designed to cater primarily to adolescent males, whom he argues are biologically prone to aggression. "What we have seen in the history of mass entertainment," Twitchell writes, "is that when a particular audience, primarily adolescent male, gains access to a medium and can therefore influence the stories told, the stories will become progressively more sensational. . . . This is not a recent phenomenon, although each generation thinks it is." Jeffrey Goldstein, the editor of *Why We Watch: The Attractions of Violent Entertainment*, also notes that "adolescent boys like violent entertainment more than any other group does," although he is quick to note that "not every boy and man finds images of violence enjoyable, and not every female finds them repugnant."

The Power of Film

While the ancient roots of violent entertainment are undeniable, many critics believe that film and television present a more visceral vision of violence than books or plays are capable of. As an example of the screen's ability to affect audiences, film historians point to 1903's *The Great Train Robbery*, one of the first silent films. In the film, a bandit fires his pistol directly at the camera, and audiences at the time literally ducked for cover. Moviegoers quickly became used to this trick of cinematography, but filmmakers ever since have been devising new images to shock and frighten viewers. "Though mayhem may be the perennial stuff of fiction, film gives it a uniquely modern edge," writes book and film critic Peter Jukes. "From the Lumiere brothers' first trick of terrifying their spectators with an oncoming express train, the camera has constantly probed into previously obscene extremes, showing us, close up, things we couldn't otherwise witness and survive."

Screen violence in the era of silent films, writes the *Kansas City Star*'s Robert W. Butler, "was diluted by the relative primitiveness of the moviemaking process." In the 1930s and '40s, the Hollywood Production Code—a set of voluntary standards that film studios were expected to conform to—prohibited graphic displays of bloodshed. But as early as 1953 the western *Shane* began pushing the code's boundaries. In one shocking scene, writes Butler, a farmer is shot and "lifted off his feet by the bullet, flung backward and sent sliding across a muddy street as if by a cannon. Audiences had never seen anything like it."

In the 1960s, filmmakers began ignoring the code, and in 1966 it was revised to give directors more discretion in how they portrayed violence. In 1967 *Bonnie and Clyde*—"the movie that rewrote the book on film violence," according to Butler—became the first to feature graphic depictions of gunshot wounds. At the film's end the title characters are killed in a hail of gunfire. A year later director Sam Peckinpah's *The Wild*

Bunch ended with a similarly fatal shootout, but in Peckinpah's film more characters are killed and the violence is shown in slow motion.

In addition to slow motion, later filmmakers added other "special effects" to enhance their depictions of violence. Squibs—exploding capsules of fake blood—allowed filmmakers to simulate bloody gunshot wounds. In the late 1970s and '80s makeup artists began using latex, a plastic material made to look like human skin, to simulate increasingly gory wounds and bodily mutilations. In the 1990s, digitized computer effects allowed filmmakers to simulate the destruction of whole cities, as in 1996's *Independence Day*, and to film more elaborate gun battles than ever before, as in 1999's *The Matrix*.

The Pervasiveness of Television

Film is the medium in which the most shockingly violent images have appeared, but television is the medium that has made violent imagery more prevalent than ever before. Television has given most American children access to endless hours of increasingly violent programming that simply did not exist before the 1950s. From the 1960s through the 1980s, children's cartoons were notoriously violent; since the 1990s, however, networks have been careful to limit the violence in children's cartoons. Fistfights, car chases, and shootouts, on the other hand, remain staples of television crime dramas that young people often are allowed to watch. It has been estimated that the average American will witness approximately twenty thousand simulated television deaths in his or her lifetime.

Critics argue that this amount of violent imagery must have a negative effect on child development. Television "has absorbed much of the socializing function of parents, schools, and churches," writes Mary Ann Watson, the author of *Defining Visions: Television and the American Experience Since 1945*. "From the home screen, we've all derived lessons about what society expects from us and notions about what we expect from society." In her opinion, saying "If you don't like what's on TV, just turn it off," is like saying "If you're troubled by air pollution, just stop breathing."

Because of the pervasiveness of television, much of the scientific research on media violence has focused on television violence. In general the research indicates that heavy viewing of television violence is associated with increased aggression and other antisocial effects (although it is difficult to determine whether violent entertainment makes people aggressive or whether aggressive people are more drawn to violent entertainment).

Violence in Popular Culture

Violence is a prominent theme in many types of entertainment besides film and television. In many cases this is simply because drama involves conflict, and conflict often involves violence. But for almost every form of popular entertainment, there are genres defined by their preoccupation with violence.

The book publishing industry has the violent horror of authors like Stephen King and Dean R. Koontz, the military thrillers of authors such as Tom Clancy, and the perennially popular murder mystery. The music industry has gangsta rap, which since the early 1990s has been continually attacked for its glorification of guns and violence against women, and shock rockers such as Marilyn Manson, who have been accused of promoting suicide and self-mutilation. In the world of professional sports, boxing, football, and hockey are often called "blood sports," and the over-the-top violence of professional wrestling consistently draws audiences.

One form of entertainment that has often been singled out as being too violent is video games. Since the 1980s, when they began moving from arcades into the home via computers and game consoles, video games have become more popular, and parents have become more concerned about their content. As with other media, not all video games are violent, but some video game genres do center around violence. There are war strategy games and martial-arts-style fighting games, but the most violent genre is that of the first-person shooter, which essentially allows the player to simulate the shootouts that are so prominent in violent films and television. First-person shooter video games such as *Doom* and *Quake* were drawn into the media violence debate after the media reported that Eric Harris and Dylan Klebold, the two teenagers who shot thirteen people at their Littleton, Colorado, high school in April 1999, had played them.

The growing concern over violent video games is very similar to the debates over film and television violence. As with film, video games have become increasingly violent as they have become more popular and profitable. And as with television, many young children have access to video games at home. They may spend many hours playing a single violent game, and thus view many incidents of fictional violence just as a heavy viewer of television crime dramas would. The term *screen violence* is sometimes used to encompass film, television, and video game violence.

Examining Screen Violence

The debate over media violence tends to run in cycles. Controversy erupts after a tragedy such as the one in Littleton, Colorado, and critics focus on a particularly violent film, television show, or video game. Eventually the public loses interest, only to have the cycle repeated months or years later after another shockingly violent crime makes the headlines. Each time, the debate seems new and specific to current trends in popular culture that may have influenced those who committed the violence.

The essays in *Examining Pop Culture: Violence in Film and Television* attempt to take a broader view, recognizing that violence has been a prominent theme in movies and television since their inception. The first group of essays in this volume examines the major violent film genres. Another group of essays summarizes the research that has been conducted on television violence. In the final two groups of essays, authors debate how serious the problem of media violence is and examine various ways of dealing with the issue. By exploring screen violence in detail, it is hoped that the reader will better understand why violence is such an enduring, controversial, and complex theme in popular culture.

EXAMINING POP CULTURE

Violent Film Genres

A Brief History of Film Violence

Stephen Prince

In 1930, in response to growing concerns over movie content, the major film studios agreed to adhere to the Hollywood Production Code, which regulated what types of violence could be shown on screen. By the 1960s, however, the Motion Picture Association of America relaxed the code's guidelines to give filmmakers more freedom. The looser restrictions, coupled with the invention of "squibs" (exploding capsules of fake blood), paved the way for bloodier death scenes in films such as *A Fistful of Dollars* and *Bonnie and Clyde*. In the 1970s innovations in special effects allowed filmmakers to portray increasingly graphic scenes of gore. By the 1990s, graphic violence had become such a regular feature of mainstream Hollywood films that filmmakers used it for stylistic or comedic effect in films like *Pulp Fiction*.

Stephen Prince is a professor of communication studies at Virginia Tech and the author of several books, including *Savage Cinema: Sam Peckinpah and the Rise of Ultraviolent Movies*. The following essay is adapted from Prince's introduction to *Screening Violence*, an anthology on cinema violence.

VIOLENCE IN THE MOVIES IS NOT OF RECENT origin. Screen violence is deeply embedded in the history and functioning of cinema. It is as old as the medium and has arguably been of central importance for the popular appeal of

■

film. Edwin Porter's *The Great Train Robbery* (1903) shows a beating victim (albeit transmuted into a none-too-convincing dummy) thrown from a moving train and climaxes with a massacre of the train robbers. D.W. Griffith's *Intolerance* (1916) shows decapitation and other gruesome sights and climaxes, as did many of his pictures, with thrilling scenes of physical action. The appeal of violence in cinema—for filmmakers and viewers—is tied to the medium's inherently visceral properties. These make the cinema especially suited to the depiction of violence. Brian De Palma, a well-known contemporary exponent of movie violence, has noted this fundamental connection between the plastic components of the medium and the emotional pleasures it offers. "Motion pictures are a kinetic art form; you're dealing with motion and sometimes that can be violent motion. There are very few art forms that let you deal with things in motion and that's why Westerns and chases and shoot-outs crop up in film. They require one of the elements intrinsic to film: motion."

The Hollywood Production Code

Although movie violence has a long history, in contrast with today's films, screen violence in earlier periods was more genteel and indirect. From 1930, when it was formulated, until the 1960s, Hollywood's Production Code regulated all aspects of screen content, with an elaborate list of rules outlining what was permissible to show and what was not. These regulations placed great constraints on filmmakers and helped to prevent the emergence of ultraviolence in American film during these earlier periods. (With its decapitation [and its nudity], *Intolerance* was a pre-Code film.) In filmic depictions of crime, for example, the Code stipulated that brutal killings must not be shown in detail, murder must not be glamorized so as to inspire imitation, and the use of firearms should be sparing. This censure against excessive depictions of firearms stands in sharp contrast with the fetish for high-tech firepower in today's action films, which devote long, lingering close-ups to weapons, as cradled in the arms of Sylvester Stallone, Arnold Schwarzennegger, and other superheroes.

From 1930 on, filmmakers had to shoot and cut their material with the Code's provisions in mind because the major studios would not distribute films that lacked a Code seal of approval. Thus, explicit footage showing King Kong trampling his victims or Frankenstein's monster tossing a little girl into a lake (she drowns) was deleted from the final cuts of those pictures. And in countless Westerns and urban crime dramas, shooting victims frowned and sank gracefully out of frame, with their white shirts immaculate. . . .

The Genesis of Ultraviolence

The beginning of the shift, that point when the graphic representation of physical violence first became a distinct stylistic possibility in the American cinema, is easy to date. Ultraviolence emerged in the late 1960s, and movies have never been the same since. The factors that helped produce this new violence were instigated by two watershed events in Hollywood history: the revision in September 1966 of Hollywood's thirty-six-year-old Production Code and the creation two years later of the Code and Rating Administration with its G-M-R-X classification scheme. These changes were responses to the more liberal and tolerant culture of the period, particularly the revolution in social mores tied to the youth movement. Shackled by the Production Code, movies were thirty years behind the times. Accordingly and led by the Motion Picture Association of America (MPAA), the Hollywood industry mounted an aggressive campaign to make films relevant again for a society whose attitudes and practices no longer coincided with the morality institutionalized in the Production Code.

Thus, the 1966 revision scrapped the Code's injunctions about specific content areas and substituted in their place a few broadly phrased guiding principles that, as MPAA head Jack Valenti pointed out, significantly expanded the creative license of filmmakers. Where the old Code told filmmakers precisely how they were to approach and show scenes of violence, the revised Code merely recommended that filmmakers exercise discretion in showing the taking of human life. "Discretion" is an elastic and relative concept, and as the intensifying violence in American cinema in the late 1960s shows, it was mostly an ineffective principle. But the scrapping of specific content injunctions was not the most significant revision. In a development that was far more important and influential for subsequent filmmaking, the MPAA created a new Suggested for Mature Audiences (SMA) designation for films that had harder, more adult content. This new designation enabled filmmakers for the first time to target an adult audience and on that basis take sex and violence much further than in the past when the audience mix included young viewers.

An additional revision a few years later accelerated these developments. In 1968, the MPAA unveiled a four-way classification system—G-M-R-X—that differentiated films by audience segment. G-rated films were suitable for the entire family, while underage viewers were prohibited from seeing X-rated films and could only view R-films if accompanied by a parent or adult guardian. The G-M-R-X scheme made even greater freedoms available to filmmakers because films could now be niche-marketed to adult audiences, bypassing the content restrictions that the presence of young viewers had hitherto necessitated. These modifications of the Production Code helped produce a wave of tougher, harder-edged, and controversial films whose graphic violence, profanity, and sexuality exemplified the new artistic freedoms that the MPAA had been seeking and promoting. Films like *Bonnie and Clyde* (1967), *The Fox* (1968), *The Detective* (1968), *In Cold Blood* (1967), *Point Blank* (1967), and *Barbarella* (1968) would have been unthinkable a mere five years previously, and they collectively demonstrate the emergence of the new, adult-themed cinema that the MPAA helped inaugurate. . . .

A Cultural Fascination with Violence

A 1968 MPAA audience survey showed that 16- to 24-year-olds were responsible for 48 percent of national ticket sales. To capture this young audience, the MPAA believed that films would have to become more attuned to contemporary mores, which adherence to a thirty-six-year-old Production Code prevented. In addition to the youth audience, however, a multitude of other factors influenced and helped shape the new direction of American cinema. The period's general social turmoil, its climate of political violence, and, most especially, the war in Vietnam convinced many filmmakers and the MPAA that movie violence paled next to the real-life bloodshed in the nation's cities and the jungles of Southeast Asia. The savage bloodshed of the Vietnam War established a context whereby filmmakers felt justified in reaching for new levels of screen violence. Moreover, the war and the political assassinations of the 1960s fed a general cultural fascination with violence to which the movies responded.

Jack Valenti remarked on the interconnections between the era's social and media violence and did so in a manner that claimed film's prerogative in responding to real-world violence. In 1968, he remarked, "For the first time in the history of this country, people are exposed to instant coverage [on television] of a war in progress. When so many movie critics complain about violence on film, I don't think they realize the impact of 30 minutes on the Huntley-Brinkley newscast—and that's real violence." *Bonnie and Clyde* was the most explicitly violent film that had yet been made, and its director, Arthur Penn, claimed that he didn't consider it especially violent when taken in context of the Vietnam era. "Not given the times in which we were living, because every night on the news we saw kids in Vietnam being airlifted out in body bags, with blood all over the place. Why, suddenly, the cinema had to be immaculate, I'll never know."

Resulting from the industry's efforts to connect with a young, contemporary audience and the period in which that audience lived, motion picture violence began its remarkable escalation in 1967. United Artists released Sergio Leone's *Dollars* trilogy of Westerns—*A Fistful of Dollars, For a Few Dollars More*, and *The Good, the Bad, and the Ugly*—on staggered dates throughout that year to accentuate the series nature of the films. Their release triggered a storm of protest over Leone's more cold-blooded and brutal depiction of the West. A reviewer for *Variety*, the film industry's trade journal, called *Fistful* a "bloodbath," with "sadism from start to finish, unmitigated brutality, a piling up of bodies." The paper's subsequent review of *The Good, the Bad, and the Ugly* objected, "One sequence in particular, a five-minute torture session that climaxes in an attempted eye-gouging, may well serve as the battle cry for opponents of screen violence."

The Leone films, which had been made in Italy, aroused considerable protest from groups opposed to the new screen violence, but it was two American films that year—*The Dirty*

Dozen and *Bonnie and Clyde*—that ignited the loudest cries. *The Dirty Dozen* was an uncommonly cynical World War II action picture about hardened criminals recruited for a suicide mission into Nazi Germany. In the climax of the picture, the Americans incinerate their Nazi enemies by locking them in closed quarters, dousing them with petrol, and setting them afire. The sadism of the sequence appalled many commentators. Among the most vocal of these was Bosley Crowther, the prominent *New York Times* critic. He condemned the film, and the new movie violence of which it was part, for its "glorification of killing" and for blatantly appealing to an audience's aggressive and sadistic appetites. *Bonnie and Clyde* went even farther by explicitly portraying the details and physicality of violent death, concluding with an extended slaughter sequence that shows the outlaws raked with automatic weapons' fire, their bodies riddled by bullet strikes. Both *Time* and *Newsweek* condemned the film as bloodthirsty trash in initial reviews, only to issue retractions in an unprecedented second round of reviews that praised the picture as trendsetting.

Slow Motion and Squibs

Indeed, Penn was the first American filmmaker to utilize the cinematic techniques that quickly became the normative means of filming violent gun battles. Taking his cue from Japanese director Akira Kurosawa, who had used these techniques in *Seven Samurai* (1954) and other films, Penn employed multicamera filming (i.e., filming with more than one camera running simultaneously), slow motion, and montage editing (i.e., building a sequence out of many, very short, brief shots). To these techniques which rendered gun violence with greater intensity than ever before, Penn added squibs. Probably more than any other effects tool, squibs changed the way screen violence looked.

Squibs were condoms filled with fake blood, concealed within an actor's clothing, and wired to detonate so as to simulate bullet strikes and blood sprays. Squibs enabled filmmakers to graphically visualize the impact of bullets on the human body, a detailing that is absent in film prior to 1967 and which helped give violence in these earlier periods an unreal and sanitized appearance. To be sure, certain pictures in these earlier periods anticipated the modern staging of gun violence. In *Shane* (1953), for example, a gunfire victim is hurled backward by the force of a bullet's impact, and in Penn's own *The Left-Handed Gun* (1958), a hapless deputy is literally blown out of his boot by a gun blast. But despite such striking details, these scenes lacked squib-work and the palpable physicality that it lent gun violence. During and after 1967, by contrast, the savage impact of gunfire on human flesh became an enduring feature of screen killing. Films released in the same year as *Bonnie and Clyde* and which lacked squib-work—*The Professionals*, *El Dorado*—seemed bloodless, irrevocably part of a now-archaic era in screen violence and not at all contemporary with Penn's film. In the film's climactic sequence, Bonnie (Faye Dunaway) and Clyde (Warren Beatty) are ambushed by the Texas Rangers, who are armed with machine guns. The actors were rigged with multiple squibs. When detonated in sequence and augmented by the writhing of the actors, these provided a horrifying visualization of the outlaws' bodies being punctured by scores of bullets. . . .

The Wild Bunch

The outstanding commercial success of Leone's *Dollars* trilogy, *The Dirty Dozen*, and *Bonnie and Clyde* showed that the public had hitherto unappeased appetites for screen carnage and that the industry could make a lot of money from filming hyperviolence. Thus, in short order, the threshold that *Bonnie and Clyde* had crossed in 1967, with its images of slow-motion bloodletting, was surpassed. Director Sam Peckinpah's *The Wild Bunch* (1969) offered two extended slaughter sequences, opening and closing the film, that were far more gruesome, graphic, and protracted than the gun battle in Penn's picture had been. Nothing in the American cinema had been as remotely violent as what Peckinpah now put on screen in *The Wild Bunch*. . . .

Many viewers were appalled by the film's gore. An early test screening of the film elicited such negative responses as "The movie is nothing but mass murder" and "Nauseating, unending, offensive bloody violence." But the film also had its passionate defenders, and these included ordinary viewers as well as prominent film critics. Penn and Peckinpah were enormously talented filmmakers, and they had crafted the two most vivid, audacious, and ambitious films that Hollywood had seen in many years. Thus, these pictures gained a significant measure of respect and critical stature that helped legitimize the in-your-face bloodletting that otherwise made them so notorious. Penn and Peckinpah were both radical social critics, disturbed by the corruption of America in its Vietnam years, and they proved that filmmakers in the late 1960s could use graphic violence for serious purposes. Peckinpah, for example, repeatedly remarked that he wished to deglamorize movie violence in order to show how ugly and awful real violence was.

Unfortunately, and perhaps inevitably, the stylistics of graphic violence proved to hold tremendous fascination for subsequent generations of filmmakers who did not share Penn and Peckinpah's radical social objectives. The explicitness of this violence quickly escalated. Made only a few years after *The Wild Bunch*, for example, *Taxi Driver* (1976) was far bloodier and much more graphic, with images of dismemberment and a gunshot victim's brains splattered on a wall. Penn and Peckinpah helped establish the stylistic features of ultraviolence, while subsequent filmmakers have replicated and exaggerated them. Squib-work, multicamera filming, and montage editing utilizing differential rates of slow motion—this combination of elements became one of the two dominant aesthetic forms of ultraviolence. It is today very difficult to find gun battles in movies that have not been stylized in this fashion. (The elaborate gun battles in *L.A. Confidential* [1997] are notably deviant because they lack slow motion.) Moreover, the form has been internationalized. Hong Kong director John Woo (*The Killer* [1989], *Hard Boiled* [1992]) is the best-known contemporary exponent of the furiously bloody gun battles in the style elaborated by Penn and Peckinpah. Despite the fact that Woo's work is situated in another culture and country (at least until his current Hollywood period), the formal design of violence in his films follows the now-familiar and conventional parameters of the Penn-Peckinpah stylistic.

Gore Films

Contemporary ultraviolence exhibits a second predominant aesthetic form. In addition to the Penn-Peckinpah stylistic, ultraviolence includes graphic imagery of bodily mutilation. This type of imagery was not part of the Penn-Peckinpah stylistic, beyond the use of squib-work, because that style stressed the kinetic effects of montage, making violence balletic, a dance of death. But graphic mutilation—eye gouging, impalement, and dismemberment—surfaced in the horror film in the late 1970s and the 1980s, as that genre abandoned the atmospherics of earlier decades and offered instead stomach-churning and gut-wrenching experiences. As Carol Clover notes,

> The perfection of special effects has made it possible to show maiming and dismemberment in extraordinarily credible detail. The horror genres are the natural repositories of such effects; what can be done is done, and slashers, at the bottom of the category, do it most and worst. Thus we see heads squashed and eyes popped out, faces flayed, limbs dismembered, eyes penetrated by needles in close-up, and so on.

The genre's remarkable resurgence in the 1980s was tied to this investment in ultraviolence. The decade opened with a huge spike in horror film production, which rose from 35 pictures produced in 1979 to 70 in 1980 and 93 in 1981. Films in this spike included *Dressed to Kill*, *Friday the 13th*, *Prom Night*, and *Maniac*, all notoriously violent pictures. The genre spiked again in 1986–87, hitting a peak of 105 pictures in 1987. By mid-decade, the video market was thriving, and many of these pictures, especially the most violent and disreputable, were low-budget, throw-away entries aimed at this ancillary market.

Developments in two areas of makeup special effects, practiced by a new generation of makeup artists, stimulated the genre's turn to ultraviolence. The artists included Tom Savini (*Dawn of the Dead*, *Maniac*, *Friday the 13th*, *Eyes of a Stranger*), Rick Baker (*It's Alive*, *Squirm*, *The Funhouse*), and Rob Bottin (*The Howling*, *Piranha*, *The Thing*). These artists employed prosthetic limbs and latex (as a convincing stand-in for human skin) to simulate exquisitely detailed body mutilations. Limbs could be hacked off with a convincing show of bone and gristle, and skin (latex) could be ripped, scored, punctured, and peeled away, much to the roaring delight of audiences who patronized these films and enjoyed the new sadism.

The most controversial of the new horror pictures were

the slasher films about serial killers slaughtering promiscuous teenagers. These slaughterfests seemed to demonstrate rampant sadism in popular culture, and they disturbed many observers inside and outside the film industry. Horror film bloodfests were present in high numbers at the international film markets in 1980, the first year of the genre's big production boom. Distributors and studio sales reps expressed revulsion at these products. "All they want is blood pouring off the screen. I question the mental balance of the people making and buying this stuff," noted a Carolco executive. The imagery of victims dismembered by spikes, axes, chain saws, or power drills, or run through meat grinders evoked a swift and stern backlash from critics, especially feminist scholars, who pointed out that a basic slasher film premise was a male killer stalking and slaughtering female victims. . . .

The controversies, though, did not stop the productions, although by the late 1990s the slasher cycle was nearly played out, as evidenced in part by the degree of self-consciousness it attained in Wes Craven's *Scream* films. But ultraviolent horror films remain very popular, as the huge collections of gory movies in video stores demonstrate and as the Web pages devoted in cyberspace to Jason, Freddy Kreuger, and the other killer heroes indicate.

Ultraviolent films since 1967 have utilized these two aesthetic formats—montage-slow motion and graphic mutilation—to provide very powerful and intense experiences for spectators. The medium's power to agitate, horrify, and excite movie audiences has generated persistent concern about the psychological and social effects of violent films. These concerns have appeared throughout film (and television) history. . . .

Graphic Violence Is Now the Norm

Graphic violence is now so endemic to the medium, such a pervasive feature of contemporary style, that filmmakers have become disconnected from the carnage on which they turn their cameras. In an odd but understandable turn of events, many filmmakers who purvey ultraviolence are emotionally disengaged from it and show it in a dispassionate manner. For them, it is a special effect and a box-office asset. This is quite evident in routine action films, but it sometimes afflicts even fine directors. Oliver Stone's *Natural Born Killers* (1994), for example, plays violence as a cartoon in a disconnected, post-modern style that romanticizes the serial killers it professes to critique. Its attentive and flamboyant depictions of violence make it a part of the violence-loving media it aims to target. Most of the ultraviolence in *Pulp Fiction* is played as comedy, with no grounding in suffering or pain. Cinematographer John Bailey has remarked that "the artifice of movie mayhem" has become "routine and unreal to us as filmmakers."

This unreality is symptomatic of the social disconnect of many contemporary filmmakers. For them, violence is an image to be constructed, a special effect to be staged, but not a social effect that is produced. When characters die spectacularly bloody deaths in contemporary crime and action films, they are, for the individuals who make these films, just movie characters, without real-life correlates. In the culture of ultraviolence that now engulfs the medium, moviemakers operate in a kind of postmodern bubble, treating violence as an image and not as a social process. Furthermore, the sheer pervasiveness of media violence helps augment this sense of unreality. It has become an object for consumption, a familiar part of the social landscape as defined by movies and television. As German director Wim Wenders has said, "Violence appears in so many contexts where you cannot reflect on it any more, where you cannot experience it any other way than consuming."

Violence has a legitimate place in art as part of the human experience and as one of the mysteries of life that haunts and fascinates. But viewers rarely experience screen violence in this fashion, treated in a serious and provocative way that invites reflection and contemplation (and, as noted, the medium of cinema does not make this kind of depiction easy to achieve). Instead, commercial films offer it as spectacle, an easy way to get to the viewer emotionally and to solve narrative issues. And it all becomes ever more unreal, ever more stylized and disconnected from a viewer's personal experience, except, as the empirical studies suggest, for its impact on the social psychology of the culture. There seems, at present, no way out from the blood and circus that much of present cinema has become, especially as the culture at large manifests such fascination (albeit horrified) with an ongoing spate of headline-grabbing homicides. The Littleton shootings were recent instances in a lengthy spate of murders in which the killers had feasted on media ultraviolence. In the words of a teenager sentenced to life for killing his mother, "The first stage you see a guy's head being blown off and you feel compassion. The second stage you see it again, you feel compassion, but it's not as strong as the first . . . the fifth stage, you want to do it but it's just a thought. The last stage you do it and you want to do it again." Certainly this killer's words are self-serving. But they also speak to a worst-case, nightmare scenario about the connections between ultraviolent movies and real violence.

Once American cinema turned the corner toward graphic violence, there has been no going back. And the culture as a whole has accompanied cinema on this journey, becoming bloodier, ever more grim, and ever more confused about the accelerating spiral of movie-induced carnage.

Teen Rebellion Films and Juvenile Delinquency

David M. Considine

David M. Considine is the author of *The Cinema of Adolescence*, from which the article below is excerpted. In it he describes the juvenile delinquency scare of the 1950s and the cycle of films that both exploited and fueled public concern about violent teenagers. Juvenile delinquency rose throughout the first half of the 1950s, and as early as 1953 critics worried that films like *Teenage Menace* not only portrayed wayward youth, but might also incite young viewers to violence. In 1954 and 1955, *The Wild One*, *East of Eden*, and *Rebel Without a Cause*, which all centered around alienated young men, came to define a new genre: the teen rebellion film. Early teen rebellion films such as *The Blackboard Jungle* attempted to explore seriously the causes of juvenile delinquency, but after the success of the 1961 musical *West Side Story*, filmmakers turned away from serious depictions of teen angst in favor of more stylized, less gritty portrayals of juvenile violence.

THROUGHOUT THE 1950'S JUVENILE DELIN-quency went from a social reality to a national obsession and nothing or no one was more obsessed than the media. Senator Kefauver's investigation into juvenile crime received national attention. The media, particularly motion pictures, represented in the fifties a site of, a source for, and a stimulus to juvenile delinquency.

■

Excerpted from *The Cinema of Adolescence*, by David M. Considine (Jefferson, NC: McFarland, 1985). Copyright © David M. Considine, 1985. Used with permission.

With the decade just under way provocative headlines brought the new menace sharply to the public's attention. [A 1950 article from *Colliers* magazine began:]

> When ten-year-olds carry guns; when youngsters 13 to 17 pummel innocent pedestrians with black jacks or lay open their cheeks with rings filed sharp as scalpels; when young wolf packs roam the streets for prey; when they flail their victims with chains and belts, smash at them with brass knuckles or fists weighted with lead; when kids who are still wet behind the ears worship a new god named violence, the city must sit up and take notice.

Between 1945 and 1948 juvenile delinquency, which had grown to alarming proportions during the war years, began to decline, reaching a low of 300,000 cases. By 1949 it was on the rise again. In 1953 the number of cases had climbed to 435,000 and by 1955 it had hit the half million mark. The cinema was not immune to the effects of this outburst of adolescent crime. In November 1953, *Variety* reported:

> Vandalism in theaters, a serious problem since the end of World War II, continues unabated to the extent that theater-men in various sections of the country regard it as a greater menace than television. . . . While the degree of vandalism varies in different sections of the country, it is a nationwide problem. Educators, civic authorities and social workers point out that it is not confined only to theaters but that vandalism extends to the streets, the parks, the schools and even the housing developments where the youngsters reside.

Juvenile Delinquency Goes to the Movies

Not only was the cinema the scene of juvenile crime, it was increasingly seen as a stimulus to such crime. In 1953 Dr. Hugh Flick, director of the motion picture division of the New York State Education Department, refused to license *Teenage Menace* on the grounds that it would incite crime. In September 1954 *Variety* reported that New York Police believed films depicting crooked cops fostered disrespect for the law, made the job of policemen more difficult, and served as a "juve crime aid." Yet despite such comments, concerns and controversy, from 1954 on Hollywood embarked upon a deliberate policy of depicting juvenile delinquency. No period before and no period since has seen such a sustained and systematic attempt to court the adolescent audience by the sensationalized depiction of teenage crime and waywardness.

At a time when Frankie Lymon and the Teenagers sang "I'm Not a Juvenile Delinquent," the movies seemed to be going out of their way to suggest that among American youth, delinquency, rather than being the exception, was the rule. From the mid-fifties on, theaters were inundated by low budget B movies employing sensationalism and exploitation to capture the expanding teenage market. With their parents firmly ensconced at home with their eyes glued to the television set, adolescents escaped to the drive-ins and the movie theaters that fulfilled their fantasies.

At home on the small screen, the parents of middle America had their own fantasies fulfilled. While tabloids and Washington committees harangued them with tales of youthful excess and abandon, television served to placate their fears. Ozzie and Harriet never seemed to have trouble with David and Ricky. In *Father Knows Best* Jim and Margaret Anderson managed to raise Betty, Bud and Kathy without the intervention of the police and the courts. Wally and the Beaver, under the watchful eyes of Ward and June Cleaver, stuck to the straight and narrow. When delinquency did find its way to television, it was usually part of an anthology series such as Reg Rose's *Tragedy in a Temporary Town* or Robert Alan Arthur's *Man Is Ten Feet Tall*.

But on the big screens the silent generation increasingly encountered images of themselves as turbulent young people from dislocated homes. Roger Corman, American International Pictures, and others were not slow to realize the potential profit in catering to these kids. What followed was an avalanche of third-rate films which did nothing to further understanding between kids and their parents or between kids and the law.

In 1957 Warners offered *Teenage Thunder* and *Untamed Youth*. Allied Artists provided *Hot Rod Rumble*. From the AIP stable came *Motorcycle Gang* and *Dragstrip Girl*. 1958 saw Republic's *Juvenile Jungle*, Allied's *Hot Car Girl* and *Joy Ride*. When AIP released *The Cool and the Crazy*, *Hollywood Reporter* was prompted to comment:

A few weeks ago a Brooklyn school principal committed suicide because he could not suppress the rape and hooliganism in his institution. *The Cool and the Crazy* is a badly written, poorly directed, low-budget film that may well inspire more such tragedies.

Depictions of Wayward Youth

. . . In 1954 two major films emerged which were to have a profound impact on Hollywood's depiction of adolescence, not only for the rest of the decade but for years to come. Although Marlon Brando and the bike riders of *The Wild One* appear to be out of their teens, the film itself, by its antiestablishment, poor-misunderstood-kid stance, served the double function of attracting adolescents while appalling adults. As the inarticulate and mumbling Johnny, Brando etched a caricature of youth which long outlived the era that created it. The Black Rebels Motorcycle Gang, like urban outlaws riding their chrome and steel stallions through the rural hamlets of middle America, proclaim that the times are changing. And yet though the gang has strength and power, a theme already seen in *City Across the River*, they have no idea how to channel it or use it. In 1944 the *Saturday Evening Post* had asked, "Are We Raising Another Lost Generation?" In the character of Johnny and those like him the answer appears to be a decided yes. While the film was seen by many to be a glorification of violence and aggression, it was equally about alienation and a dreadful anger when generations collide but cannot communicate.

While the threat of violence creates tension which pervades the film, the story and the script also incessantly hammer away at the theme of aimlessness. *Variety* called Johnny "a hard-faced hero who never knew love as a boy." His uncertainty and his search for kicks seems to stem unconsciously from his desire to be loved. His relationship with Mary bears out this awkward, wretched need. Wanting to reach out, he is at the same time intent upon appearing strong. In such a situation, feelings for a female render him vulnerable and the relationship becomes ambiguous.

Rather than being confined to this movie, the nature of the relationship between Johnny and Mary was repeated elsewhere throughout the decade. Brando and Eva Marie Saint depicted it in *On the Waterfront* the same year. *East of Eden*, also a product of 1954, found James Dean and Julie Harris in a not unsimilar role. The reaching out is always accompanied by a drawing away from and a profound sense of uncertainty and confusion. "I don't think you know what you're trying to do or how to go about getting it," the sheriff tells Johnny. "You're afraid of me," Mary tells him. "You're still fighting, aren't you? You're always fighting. Why do you hate everybody?" He is in fact the rebel without a cause, the angry young man in a hurry but with nowhere to go and life reduced to an endless search for kicks. Asked what he's rebelling against, his response is simple: "What have you got?"

In *Rebel Without a Cause*, Jim and Buzz stand overlooking the bluff before the chicken race. Locked into ritual and routine, neither boy understands why they must do this thing, only that there seems nothing else to do. Like Johnny's, theirs is a rebellion for rebellion's sake, because in the empty silence of post-war America, the mediocre and the mundane have become the order of the day. "What are they fighting about?" a character asks. The answer: "I don't know, they don't know themselves, probably." In the end, faced with Korea, the bomb, and the prospect of ultimate annihilation, these kids can think of no greater question than "what do you do around here for kicks?" When the answer is nothing, it's time to kick out and kick up. . . .

Blaming Parents

In the thirties Hollywood had suggested that delinquency grew out of a combination of factors including economic conditions, the environment, and family life. The forties, particularly in films like *Mildred Pierce* and *Knock on Any Door*, raised the haunting possibility that such conditions were too ingrained in the social fabric to be eradicated. If society was sick, and film noir seemed to suggest just that, then kids could be excused for just about anything. It was such a point of view that was increasingly evident throughout the 1950's. Unable to confront society as a whole, the film industry zeroed in on the family and on parents in particular as the source of juvenile delinquency. While parental scapegoats were hardly a new target for filmmakers, they were singled out for blame as they had been in no other period. *East of Eden*, *Rebel Without a Cause*, and *The Young Stranger* [1957] were among the best films to portray such a vision of life. The image they defined seemed to etch itself indelibly into Hollywood consciousness, pervading almost every film throughout the fifties that dealt with the topic of delinquency. . . .

In *Dino* [1957], Sal Mineo played a thirteen-year-old killer, "a kid who'll punch you in the mouth if you say hello to him." But the boy, argued the film, is not really to blame. His problems stemmed from his father who beat him even on his birthday and left him with a profound sense of worthlessness. Streetwise but desperately in need of love and understanding, Dino is left asking, "How come nobody ever kissed me? He never took me nowhere. He never fooled around with me or gave me bearhugs."

Compulsion (1959) was based on the Leopold and Loeb case and concerned itself with two youths who coldbloodedly murder a young boy. But again the problem was clearly parental. Dean Stockwell, who had been memorable as the haunting nature boy in *The Boy With Green Hair* (1948) and the impish rascal in *Kim* (1950), made the transition to screen adolescence by playing a boy immensely disturbed by his family life. "I have very little in common with my father or my mother," he admits. Despite the disturbing nature of his crime, not to mention an attempted rape, the boy is sympathetically referred to as "a sick frightened child."

When the fifties did not place the burden of guilt at the feet of parents it argued, often eloquently, on behalf of young people. *The Blackboard Jungle* [1955] saw its angry adolescents as the products of a social process and a new age. A policeman tells us, "They were five or six years old in the last war. Father in the army, mother in a defense plant, no home life, no church life, no place to go. They formed street gangs. Maybe the kids of today are like the rest of the world—mixed up, suspicious, scared. I don't know; but I do know this, gang leaders are taking the place of parents.". . .

In *Crime in the Streets* [1955] James Whitmore served as the voice of the new liberalism. "We're not talking about wild animals, we're talking about tough angry kids. You can beat 'em up—they just get tougher and angrier. Try to understand, try to remember, kids don't get tough without good reason.

We listen, we sympathize, we talk; you can't tell a kid to be good. He's got too many reasons to be bad. So we're patient and every now and then we get to one of the really wild ones. But you know, everybody expects it to happen all at once."

Exploiting a Social Issue for Profit

But in the fifties, at least as Hollywood saw it, things did seem to happen all at once. The bobby-soxer boom surrendered to the decade of the delinquent. The pleasant middle-class families that were prevalent throughout the forties were suddenly dislocated by deep trauma. Crime and delinquency, which had been almost a working-class monopoly, suddenly engulfed middle America. Hollywood was certainly not alone in discovering delinquency or providing it with a public forum. In 1955 *Life* proclaimed "Teen-Age Terror in New York Streets." In 1957 they headlined "Teen-ager Burst of Brutality." In the following year *Look* asked, "Can Tough Cops Beat the Wild Kids?" and in the same month reported on "Teen-Age Trouble." Gangs like the Enchanters, the Dragons, and the Seminoles found their names and exploits splashed across the popular press with photographs that served to bring these frightening apparitions of adolescents gone awry forcibly to the attention of the American public.

And yet while Hollywood merely followed suit, expanding on a controversial theme and pocketing the profit, in the process they once again rendered disservice to the majority of American youth. As *Readers Digest* observed in August 1956, "lurid publicity about a tiny minority of teenaged delinquents has blinded us to the solid achievements and ideals of typical American youngsters." The Camp Fire Girls, the 4-H clubs, and the Boy and Girl Scouts provided little in the way of dramatic format for either the film industry or the mass media as a whole. Bad news sold and throughout the decade Hollywood reveled in it. Even westerns like *The Left Handed Gun* succumbed to the image of the juvenile delinquent as Paul Newman played Billy the crazy mixed-up kid. . . .

As the sixties commenced the delinquency genre was dying. *Let No Man Write My Epitaph* (1960) explored the impact of parents and the environment on the adolescent as it watched Tony Romano maturely sidestepping winoes, skid-row bums and hopheads while looking for a few cc's of delerium. In 1961 John Frankenheimer directed *The Young Savages*, based upon a novel by Evan (*The Blackboard Jungle*) Hunter. Set in the teeming tenement of New York City, it concentrated on the rivalry between Italian and Puerto Rican street gangs. Three of the cast members actually had police records in the city. Members of local gangs were recruited to play feature and supporting roles. Police were so concerned at the possibility of violence during filming that the actual rumble scenes had to be shot in the less volatile climate of Hollywood.

Studio publicity described it as a story of "the young and the damned who grow in the cracks of the concrete jungle." It is a harsh, raw vision of life with teenage murderers and adolescent whores. But despite the attempts at authenticity the film fell flat and resorted to cliches. Burt Lancaster played the prosecutor who had himself struggled out of the slums. . . . Despite authentic locations and tough kids the film failed to deliver anything new or important. *Time* called the plot "make believe from the pasteboard jungle of Hollywood."

In a graphic indication of the industry's failure to respond to the issue, *Variety* wrote:

> Juvenile crime is of course a very real, ticklish issue begging for attention. . . . It is rich ripe dramatic pasture for thoughtful creative minds and a source of some concern for all Americans, especially those in large cities who come into contact with the problem just by heading down the wrong street at the wrong time.
>
> (*The Young Savages*) fails to arrive at any novel insight into the environmental mess nor does it approach the subject with fully methodological logic or calculating objectivity required by the dramatic job it sets out to do. Instead it gets waylaid with a number of familiar stereotypes, cliches and convenient oversights, and eventually resolves the issue by pinning the blame for an unquestionably heinous crime on that old reliable whipping boy, society itself.

West Side Story

The urban ghetto was also the focus of another 1961 gang vehicle, *West Side Story*. The film marked the death knoll of the delinquent films. Hugely successful, it marked the transition from reality to romance as violence became choreographed and stylized. The panorama of pain that had pushed these youngsters over the edge was submerged in a glamorized albeit bitingly satirical presentation. Many of the songs were themselves forceful. Mateship, camaraderie and communality were graphically celebrated by the Jets' proclaiming that acceptance by them into the group meant not only "You got brothers around" but, in fact, "you're a king."

In the song, "Officer Krupke," the kids make mock of the courts, parents, police and social workers. The concerns, issues and plots that had been part and parcel of Hollywood's depiction of the delinquent are reduced to cliches to be laughed at.

Writing in *The New Republic*, Stanley Kaufman suggested that in *West Side Story* audiences got to see for the first time street gangs as they really were. But there seems to be an enormous gap between the Jets and the Sharks and the gang members of *The Blackboard Jungle*, *The Young Savages*, or even the Dead End Kids. The characters in *West Side Story* are too allegorical, too one-dimensional and too contrived. Ultimately they function as cliches rather than characters. They are too neatly categorized under their little headings as the offspring of drunks, junkies and whores. Too much is taken for granted in their plea, "We ain't no delinquents, we're misunderstood, deep down inside us there is good." . . .

The End of the Delinquency Cycle

West Side Story, in romanticizing delinquency, made it commercially successful and palatable to the adult film goer's appetite. In the process it also served to alienate those young people who had looked upon such themes and subject matter as their own private property. In sweeping the Oscars, the film moved delinquency from the precincts of a subculture to popular culture, from a B movie cult to spectacular success in both the national and international markets. But it would be wrong to credit or blame this one film for the demise of the delinquency genre.

Between 1954 and 1959 Hollywood had saturated audiences with stories either totally or partially centered around delinquents. The life span of the cycle was coming to a natural conclusion by the time the sixties got under way. No period between 1930 and 1980 has been able to successfully cultivate a delinquency cycle that lasted longer than seven years; the longest period terminated with *West Side Story*. Social as well as cinematic factors also explain the end of the era. Peace and prosperity had provided the adolescents who grew out of the post-war baby boom with affluence and leisure time that had been denied their counterparts in the thirties and forties.

Action-Revenge Films

Jake Horsley

Jake Horsley is the author of a two-part volume on film criticism entitled *The Blood Poets: A Cinema of Savagery, 1958–1999*. In this excerpt from the second part of that work, *Millennial Blues: From* Apocalypse Now *to* The Matrix, Horsley examines the "action-revenge" genre of films, using the 1988 film *Die Hard* as an example. Horsley maintains that *Die Hard* and movies like it, such as the *Dirty Harry* films of the 1970s, send a message that killing the "bad guys" is morally just. Moreover, action movies deliberately build up in the audience a desire to see the villains punished. As Horsley writes, the action film "both fosters and answers *a lust for blood*." Finally, since the heroes in action movies are typically portrayed as loving husbands and fathers, action films present violence as wholesome family entertainment.

IF, AS DIRTY HARRY CALLAGHAN SAID (IN CLINT Eastwood's sleazy *Sudden Impact*), "Revenge is the oldest motivation known to mankind," then for the action movie, it may just be the oldest and most trusty plot-device there is. The "blood thriller," from *The Big Heat* to *Die Hard*, has been one of Hollywood's favorite staples of entertainment, partially because, apart from the opportunity such films provide for explosive action, the Revenge Fantasy exploits a basic (male) desire of audiences to "get dirty." The Revenge Fantasy assumed its modern guise roughly in the early '70s, with *Dirty Harry*,

■

Walking Tall and, most crucially of all, *Death Wish*. Both *Dirty Harry* and *Walking Tall* were police thrillers in which the battle for justice (as in *The Big Heat*) became just a little *too* personal to constitute orthodox police work; these films were so popular that they started a spate of renegade cop movies that has become, for the '90s moviegoer, familiar to the point of contempt. From Eastwood, Steve McQueen, Burt Reynolds, and Gene Hackman, all the way up to Arnold Schwarzenegger, Sylvester Stallone, Mel Gibson, Kevin Costner, Bruce Willis, Keanu Reeves, Nicolas Cage, etc., etc., it's hard to think of an American leading man who *hasn't* at some point in his career played the maverick lawman with a tendency to take things personally. Many of the top box office stars of the day have even made a career out of variations on just such a stereotype. Anger is perhaps the easiest thing of all for an actor to play effectively, while revenge fantasies are almost invariably popular with audiences, as the tough, brutal but "sensitive" lawman is both flattering to the "orgastically impotent" male ego, and arousing to female libidos. All in all, playing cops on a revenge mission is the easiest possible route to fame and fortune that an actor could hope for. It's also his best way to *stay* in business once he's made it—witness Eastwood's seemingly endless, progressively more lackadaisical, returns to the genre, despite the fact that it's depressingly plain to everyone that he's "too old for this shit."

The fact that a personal incentive on the part of the lawman is essential to the tawdry, relentless intensity of the cop thriller (as distinct from the ordinary police drama) may have led to the idea—on the part of movie producers—of doing away with "the line of duty" and highlighting this personal element, thereby accentuating the hitherto incidental violence, to the extent that it became the whole raison d'être of the film. . . .

Die Hard and the Modern Action Film

Bruce Willis's sculpted muscular physique is the all-too solid center of John McTiernan's *Die Hard* (1988), probably the slickest, most spectacular and enjoyably mindless action movie of the '80s, and, for the most part, one of the least offensive as well. John McClane, the New York cop played by Willis, is—true to the trusty fish-out-of-water premise—attending a Los

Angeles company party on Christmas Eve in a high-rise building where his wife works. McClane (who is indeed out of his
element with yuppies and entrepreneurs) is washing up in the
bathroom when the party is unexpectedly gate-crashed by a
group of German terrorists, led by the suavely odious Alan
Rickman. McClane manages to sneak off unnoticed while the
terrorists are gathering the hostages together and, barefoot
and in his fetching white vest, he proceeds to single-handedly
terminate the terrorists' operation, with extreme prejudice,
naturally. *Die Hard* is not a revenge-driven fantasy however,
and McClane actually *kills* amazingly few people, considering
the amount of mayhem and destruction which he causes.
There *is* a personal element involved, however—Alan Rickman's fiendishly civilized psycho is so charismatic a bad guy
that he and McClane cannot help but strike up a kind of acid
repartee (even though they communicate for most of the film
by walkie-talkie); and obviously, McClane gets to kill him in
the most lingeringly satisfying manner. But *Die Hard* is—until
the last moment at least—a surprisingly good-spirited action
movie, and the only revenge-driven character in the film is in
fact the heavy: a long blond-haired German *übermensch* [su-
perman] whose brother is McClane's first (and accidental) victim, and is so driven by hatred and rage that it even carries him
beyond the grave to get back at McClane (and to provide the
standard, shock ending while he's at it). McClane, for his part,
is motivated merely by his own sense of duty as a policeman;
he even tries throughout the film to call in outside help and to
escape from the whole mess, pointless as this is (he obviously
doesn't know the rules of the genre: the reluctant hero cannot
escape his destiny).

Once again, *Die Hard* gives us the lone maverick soldier
fighting against organized forces of evil with nothing but his
wits and his guts (and his arsenal) to even the odds. One in-
teresting thing about *Die Hard* is that McClane has more than
just the terrorists to worry about. On the inside, there's an ab-
surdly slimy, cocaine-snorting yuppie who attempts to make a
deal with the terrorists, to help them to trick McClane into
giving up, but only gets his brains blown in the process. On
the outside, there's the usual moronic police chief, combined
with the FBI, to contend with. The former rants and raves and

rails against McClane for messing things up, and for being out of his jurisdiction (by about three thousand miles), and for destroying the building (McClane blows up several floors apparently for the sheer hell of it, though he does wipe out several baddies in the process). The FBI, on the other hand, constitutes an actual threat to McClane's safety, not consciously but merely through an excess of zeal—they take him to be a terrorist and try to shoot him down. In fact *Die Hard* presents these FBI men (the script—in one of its lamer attempts at quaint humor—names them both Johnson) more or less unequivocally as bad guys. . . .

While these FBI agents are presented as rabid, trigger-happy, unethical scum (so we can cheer when they are vaporized), McClane is so "good" he even has to ask himself why he didn't save a hostage when he could have, and then tell himself, "cuz you'd be dead too," all so we know he's got a conscience, even if he's too smart to let it trip him up. (Saving the hostage in question, who is the head of the company and the first to get it, would have been no less miraculous or foolhardy a stunt than some of McClane's subsequent achievements, however.) *Die Hard* is another reactionary fable disguised as an anarchic jaunt. Granted, the FBI are baddies, but at the same time, McClane and his (black) cop buddy (whom he talks with by radio and only meets in the film's last scene) are standard macho-cop good guys, the implication being that the common lawman ethic still stands: it's only at the higher levels that things are all messed up. McClane destroys a public building and gets away with it (no one asks him any questions at the end), so you could argue that the film supports rebellious acts of vandalism and destruction of property, but if so, then it's only so far as they're necessary for the hero to prove he's tougher and crazier and more formidable than all the terrorists put together. *Die Hard*, like all Hollywood action movies, is about the triumph of "the little guy."

"The Good Wife Should Stay at Home" Bit

The action set pieces of the film have very little to do with its underlying ideology, which comes out in more deliberately planted, "subtler" moments (compared to blowing up a building, anything at all would be subtle). Specifically, there is some symbolic business concerning McClane's wife, who works for the company as vice president and uses her maiden name, in case her status as married woman might impede her advancement. McClane is personally affronted by this and starts an argument in their first scene together (the only real scene they have, in fact). She has recently been presented with a "token of appreciation" for her services—a gold Rolex, which she is reluctant to show her husband, despite the yuppie slimeball's insistence that she do so (it's a poorly staged scene, a glaringly obvious "exposé" of materialistic pettiness). Although McClane is apparently contrite at his own macho posturing and possessiveness, the film clearly supports it, as demonstrated by the last scene when his wife (of course) has to be saved by hubby from the clutches of the villain. The villain, having been shot once, is hanging out the window of the high-rise holding on to the wife's wrist, the only thing keeping him from falling to his death being—you guessed it—the gold Rolex watch. McClane duly unstraps this, thereby sending the villain straight to hell (followed directly by the watch). As the battered husband and wife emerge from the building (a police jacket wrapped around her—she's safe again in the arms of authority), the press swarm around them, and she corrects him when he describes her using her maiden name, reasserting her position as *Mrs.* McClane; having, we can only presume, seen the folly of her selfish bid for independence, and resumed her role as obedient housewife.

The film makes no apologies or excuses for such a shameful piece of hamfisted symbolism, much less for the shameless bit of propaganda. It presents it straight and without irony, as the "message" of the movie; and not the only one either, nor by any means the most dubious, which is saved for the film's very last moments.

Killing Is Good

Midway through the movie, the black cop tells a story to McClane over the radio—he shot a kid by mistake: in the dark he mistook the kid for a man and the toy pistol in his hand for a real gun. Since then, he's been unable to take his gun out of his holster. McClane makes appropriately sympathetic noises; we may wonder what the scene is doing here, save as a quick, clumsy attempt to put a lump in our throats (it's played for poignancy, and must be one of the "purest" bits of sentimental hokum ever to get stranded in an action film). If we wonder why the scriptwriters even bothered with such an obviously inappropriate piece of anti-gun propaganda, we have only to wait until the end of the movie to find out. The scene serves to set us up for an altogether different kind of propaganda: when the chief heavy comes back to life and bursts roaring out of the building like Godzilla, McClane, apparently unarmed, throws himself and his wife down to the ground; there is a shot of a pistol and the heavy falls (the harder they come.) . . . Cut back to the pistol—we wonder (if we're not thinking fast enough, and action movies *do* dull the thought processes) who it belongs to; cut to a shot of the black cop, his gun held out before him, backlit like a religious icon on a mantelpiece, an expression of wonder on his face. McClane looks up in sympathy, respect, and gratitude. By this scene, we're given to understand that the cop is "cured"—his gun is back out of his holster, he's used it right (in the line of duty) and he is a "true cop" (or real man?) again. In a word, he's remembered how to kill people without worrying about the consequences. And that seems to be the primary and central message of *Die Hard*, in the conspicuous absence of anything else (besides the "good wife should stay at home" bit) resembling a subtext. That, to paraphrase Harry Callaghan: "There's nothing wrong with killing, so long as the right people get killed."

It's messages like this that destroy one's faith in the "harmlessness" of action movies. . . .

Whetting the Audience's Appetite for Destruction

Movies above all rely on violent imagery to create a state of emotional tension and excitation, thereby making viewers vulnerable to suggestion, whereupon a certain set of values or meanings can be imposed upon them. This is evident in the way violent movies so often include extremely inappropriate and sentimental moments of grief, exaltation, or what have you (any kind of emotional outburst will do), which serve as a release for the tension created by the violent imagery. We then associate the values or meanings inherent in these "affecting" moments with *relief* (i.e., pleasure), hence identifying them as *positive* values. Often the release itself *also* involves images of violence (as in the above example from *Die Hard*) which serve as a "cleansing" or cathartic culmination to all the previous images. That's why the climax of action pictures is so important, and why the Revenge Fantasy is *the* basic model for the action movie. In it, we are given one-and-a-half hours of violent imagery, which serves to build up the suspense, emotional tension, anxiety, apprehension (and quite often rage and hatred), and only in the last moments, when the hero enacts his revenge (and so "punishes," absolves and cancels the "evil"), can our tension be released. In other words, a Hollywood Revenge Fantasy is dedicated to building up our emotions to such a state that we need and *demand* an act of violence as the only possible (and just) means to relieve our tension. The Hollywood Revenge Fantasy both instills and satisfies in us an "appetite for destruction." It both fosters and answers *a lust for blood.*

The psychological agenda of these films appears to be double-edged, however. On the one hand, they create an insatiable appetite and demand for ever more screen violence; on the other hand, paradoxically, they serve to dull our capacity to experience any emotional response to (or relief from) this violence—in a word, they operate as desensitization. This might account for the way in which the "hero" of these films has become increasingly more violent, destructive and vengeful, to the point that—in a film such as *Commando* for example—most of the film's violence is committed not by the bad guys but by the hero! This is because the desensitized audience demands more and more "righteous" or emotionally involving displays of violence. . . .

I don't think there's any question, then, that—be it through deliberate social engineering or simply cynical commercial exploitation—the spate of TV/cinema violence, while claiming to "honestly" reflect the state of the world today, is also numbing and acclimatizing us to it, without actually teaching us how to deal with it. And that youths engendered on *Die Hard* and *Rambo* movies are inevitably going to be that much more amenable to military service or what-have-you, on the one hand, and, on the other, considerably less susceptible to shock or outrage (or to conscientious objections) the next time a Gulf War or a Haitian invasion comes along (to give an extremely basic example). . . .

Killing as Family Entertainment

And of course, one thing many of these testosterone-heavy heroes have in common is that, for all their apparently sociopathic tendencies and obvious penchant for mayhem, they are, at base, upholding the status quo, defending their sacred trust. (They may be loners, even sociopaths, but at heart they believe in the very family values which they appear incapable of practicing, rather like celibate priests advocating marriage.) Mad Max is a case of the family man with nothing left to defend, and only vengeance to keep him warm. In Rambo's case, his lack of ties makes him the perfect government stoolie, the army becomes his family, war his job, and Vietnam his home. (In the second film Rambo falls for a Vietnamese girl, who is naturally killed off, so Rambo's only attachment serves, true to the action formula, to up the stakes and increase the level of justified sadism and destruction: "Now it's personal," etc.) The *Die Hard* scenario is far more typical, and to even contemplate the number of American action movies in which top-cop-rescues-wayward-wife-from-runaway-psycho, and in which the estranged couple is thereby reconciled at the end, verily boggles the mind and strains the credibility. Everybody knows Hollywood is cynically churning out remakes and sequels, but does no one notice that it's recycling the same script over and over again?

John McClane is a loving, (if ornery) old-fashioned husband and good father (we're told that his daughters miss him), and the final images of the film are of this hero leading his wife away, back into the family fold (the Great State). This family motif has a dual function. On the one hand, it legitimizes the hero, gives him heart and "soul"—we know that whatever else he is, he's also a regular guy who just wants to be able to protect his wife and bring up his kids in a safe world where Commies and terrorists and Arabs and faggots and drug addicts have no place. Hence his motives are sound. On the other hand, the family, as symbol of traditional, conservative values and conventions, is seen as being *endangered*, in need of being somehow salvaged, through the testing and proving of both the husband and the wife (and sometimes the kids, too), by exposure to the "evil" anarchic forces of chaos outside this tight family unit. In the movies, terrorism is the most standard, or typical, "evil"; hence these "forces" are seen to be literally "anarchic" or "revolutionary," and directed not only against the family but against the State as well. The parallels then become plain. When the hero saves his mate and/or offspring from the bad guy (often they all get to watch or even share a hand in the psycho's slow, painful destruction), he is reunited with them and we are given to understand that, not only was the hero justified in everything he did (i.e., killing everyone), but that it was necessary, and even beneficial, to the welfare of the family; not as individuals, but *as a unit*. The (reactionary) metaphorical message of this all-too-familiar formula is so obvious it needs little exposition. The family that slays together stays together. Family = "the people." Hero = the State that protects and serves the people (Big Brother). Evil Terrorists = the forces of anarchy, subversion, crime, nonconformity etc., that *constantly threaten the security and stability* of both the family/people and the hero/state, and therefore must at all costs be eradicated. The formula here involves not only the justification of violence and revenge but its glorification, and, finally, its popularization as "family" entertainment. It becomes another commodity—a franchise of destruction. There may be a design to the chaos, after all.

Slasher Films and Violence Against Women

Barry S. Sapolsky and Fred Molitor

In the 1970s, gore films such as *The Texas Chainsaw Massacre* set the stage for a subgenre of horror—the slasher film. *Halloween*, *Friday the 13th*, and other slasher films featured a group of teenagers being murdered, one by one, by a seemingly unstoppable stalker.

Slasher films have been widely criticized not only because of their violence, but also on the grounds that their violence is directed primarily against women. In addition it has been argued that slasher films link violence with sex. For example, a teenage girl may be shown naked or partially clothed before she is attacked. Researchers Barry S. Sapolsky of Florida State University, and Fred Molitor of California State University summarize three studies of slasher films that measured the number of scenes of violence against women, violence against men, and scenes connecting violence with sex. They conclude that while slasher films do feature scenes of extreme brutality, on the whole the violence is directed at both men and women and is not often connected to sex. They also note that in many later slasher films (perhaps in response to feminist attacks on the genre), it is often a lone surviving female who ultimately triumphs over the killer.

■

HORROR FILMS BEGAN IN THE 1930'S WITH THE release of *Dracula* and *Frankenstein*. Like modern-day slasher films, early horror films were made to attract large audiences by promising to scare them. The formula of these films worked; they became extremely popular with the public. Unlike the original horror films, slasher films use graphic violence and sexual titillation to attract audiences. To examine why the content of slasher films has changed so much from the early horror movies, we need to look briefly at the history of movies made to frighten people.

The commercial success of movies like *Dracula* was actually short lived; by the late 1940's the novelty of these types of films had worn off. After World War II, movie producers changed the object of the terror from zombies, werewolves and mummies to mammoth insects and alien beings. These science fiction horror films appealed to the public because they vented fears of nuclear war and expressed a general mistrust of science and technology.

In the 1950's the old Hollywood studio system was in decline at the same time American society was experiencing important lifestyle changes. The motion picture industry was irrevocably altered by television and teens. Television quickly grew to challenge movies as a source of entertainment for the mass audience. And foremost among the changes that would influence the production of horror films was the rise of a separate teen culture. Teenagers had money and leisure time; they soon became the core of Hollywood's audience. Film producers recognized the enormous potential market for "exploitation teenpics."

Gore Films

The 1957 movie *The Curse of Frankenstein* shocked audiences by showing blood and gore in color; teenagers loved it. Hollywood responded with a series of "horror teenpics." Most were made by independent filmmakers with relatively small budgets.

Herschell Gordon Lewis, the self-proclaimed "guru of gore," invented the "gore film" in 1963 with the release of *Blood Feast*. Made in four days and costing $24,000, *Blood Feast* differed from other horror teenpics in that it featured the stalking and mutilation of beautiful women. Lewis went on to use this successful formula to make movies such as *2000 Maniacs, Color Me Blood Red* and *The Gruesome Twosome*. In these movies, and others like them, the main attraction was scenes showing young, good-looking females being tortured and killed.

As years passed, young audiences required that gruesome images become more intense and explicit for them to become scared. Advances in special effects allowed movie-makers to satisfy viewers' insatiable appetites for dismemberment and blood. Some of these movies became much more commercially successful than others and have since reached cult status. Notable examples include *Night of the Living Dead* (1968) and *The Texas Chainsaw Massacre* (1974). In 1978, a movie called *Halloween* not only sold more tickets than any other horror film, it broke all previous box-office records for any type of film made by an independent production company.

Hollywood immediately tried to tap into the success of *Halloween*. Films such as *Friday the 13th, Don't Go In the House, Prom Night, Terror Train, He Knows You're Alone,* and *Don't Answer the Phone* were all released in 1980. All hoped to imitate the profits of *Halloween*. These movies, which are some of the first slasher films, were extremely successful. However, with their increasing popularity came strong criticism. Slasher films were condemned for frequently portraying vicious attacks against mostly females and for mixing sex scenes with violent acts.

Criticisms of Slasher Films

One condemnation of slasher movies is the widely held view that they single out women for injury and death. For example, a *Los Angeles Times* film critic claimed that the "brutal victimization of women (is) a recurring and obviously popular theme in such films." During the ABC news show *Nightline*, correspondent Gail Harris summed up slasher films as "short on plot and long on brutality and violence, much of it sexual, almost all of it directed at women." Film critics Gene Siskel and Roger Ebert made similar claims on their television program *Sneak Previews*. This assumption about the content of slasher films has also been made by social scientists who have investigated what negative effects these films might have on audiences. For example, Daniel Linz and Edward Donnerstein have consistently stated that "the victims are nearly always female" in research studies they have published on slasher films.

Slasher films have also been criticized for mixing extreme violence with sex. For example, a *New York Times* film critic has written that the violence in slasher films is "usually preceded by some sort of erotic prelude: footage of pretty young bodies in the shower, or teens changing into nighties for the slumber party, or anything that otherwise lulls the audience into a mildly sensual mood." Again, Linz and Donnerstein have shared this perception with the film critics. They have reported that slasher films often include the mutilation of women in scenes that include sexual content. It is important to know whether slasher films often portray sexual aggression. Some have claimed that mixing erotic and violent scenes causes viewers, especially males, to associate sex with aggression in their everyday lives.

Testing the Claims Made About Slasher Films

How do we know whether slasher films do portray females as victims of violence more often or repeatedly have scenes where sex is shown right before or during violence? One method of answering such questions is to take a sample of films, carefully watch them, and keep track of how many times certain events happen in each of the films viewed. This research method is called "content analysis." At least three content analyses have taken samples of slasher films and recorded whether each act of violence portrayed was performed against a male or a female character, and the number of times some type of violent behavior occurred right after or during a scene containing some element of sexuality.

G. Cowan and M. O'Brien (1990) randomly selected 56 horror movies from local video outlets and content analyzed each movie to test the assumption that females suffer most in slasher films. These researchers found no significant differences between the number of male and female victims in the sample of films. The same result was found by J.B. Weaver (1991) who examined the 10 slasher films with the highest box-office earnings through 1987. F. Molitor and B.S. Sapolsky (1993) content analyzed 30 slasher films, 10 films released in 1980, 1985 and 1989. Females were found to be no more often the victims of violence than were males. These three studies, which looked at a total of 83 different slasher films all found that, contrary to popular beliefs, females are not singled out for attack in such films.

The three content analyses found that as many males were portrayed as victims as were females, but possibly more acts of violence were being committed against females. Molitor and Sapolsky looked at the number of violent acts committed against victims. Males were found to suffer more acts of violence than did females. This finding provides further evidence which contradicts claims that females are more often the recipients of brutality in slasher films.

Molitor and Sapolsky also recorded the number of seconds male and female victims in slasher films were seen in terror, scared for their lives. Females were found to be shown in fear significantly longer than were males. The average amount of time males were seen in fear per film was under two minutes; females were seen in terror over nine minutes in the average

Terrified Women in Slasher Films

Even in [slasher] films in which males and females are killed in roughly even numbers, the lingering images are inevitably female. The death of a male is always swift; even if the victim grasps what is happening to him, he has no time to react or register terror. He is dispatched and the camera moves on. The death of a male is moreover more likely than the death of a female to be viewed from a distance, or viewed only dimly (because of darkness or fog, for example), or indeed to happen offscreen and not be viewed at all. The murders of women, on the other hand, are filmed at closer range, in more graphic detail, and at greater length.

The pair of murders at the therapy pool in *Halloween II* illustrates the standard iconography. We see the orderly killed in two shots: the first at close range in the control room, just before the stabbing, and the second as he is being stabbed, through the vapors in a medium-longshot; the slasher film. Thus, the portrayal of fear is one form of victim-ization wherein females have clearly received more attention. We will return to this point later in examining the "Final Girl."

A second, important assumption made about the content of slasher films is that violence is connected to sex. In addition to keeping track of the number of males and females killed in the sampled slasher films, each content analysis noted whether acts of violence occurred during or after sexual or erotic im-ages. The three content analyses found that scenes where sex is mixed with a female's death only occur about one time per film. Of course, murder is only one form of violence seen in slasher films. For example, a victim could be stabbed, shot or punched, and still not die. Molitor and Sapolsky found only two instances of major injury during or after a sexual display in the 30 films they examined.

The three content analyses also found that acts of sexual ag-gression are not commonly portrayed in slasher films. Cowan

orderly never even sees his assailant. The nurse's death, on the other hand, is shot entirely in medium close-up. The camera studies her face as it registers first her unwitting complicity (as the killer strokes her neck and shoulders from behind), then apprehension, and then, as she faces him, terror; we see the knife plunge into her repeatedly, hear her cries, and watch her blood fill the therapy pool. . . .

The image of the distressed female most likely to linger in memory is the image of the one who did not die: the survivor, or Final Girl. She is the one who encounters the mutilated bodies of her friends and perceives the full extent of the preceding horror and of her own peril; who is chased, cornered, wounded; whom we see scream, stag-ger, fall, rise, and scream again. She is abject terror per-sonified. If her friends knew they were about to die only seconds before the event, the Final Girl lives with the knowledge for long minutes or hours.

Carol J. Clover, "Her Body, Himself: Gender in the Slasher Film," in Stephen Prince, ed., *Screening Violence*, 2000.

and O'Brien found less than one portrayal of "forced sex" in the 56 films they examined. Weaver reports two scenes of sado-masochism as the only depictions of sexual violence in 10 slasher films. In the 30 films viewed by Molitor and Sapolsky, five occurrences of rape were observed, along with 19 instances involving a female forced to kiss and/or endure fondling against her will. Given these findings, and the rare instances wherein a female is killed during or after a sexual situation, it can be concluded that the oft-repeated claim that sex and violence are frequently linked in slasher films is unfounded.

Other Findings

Sadistic Violence. Content analyses have helped to clear up misconceptions about the images of violence and sex in slasher films. Results have shown that men suffer as often as do women, maybe more, and that when sexual images are seen, they rarely take place before or during an act of violence. There is an additional assumption made about the content of slasher films—that they contain acts of extreme violence which are portrayed in graphic detail. To ascertain the level of brutality in slasher films, Molitor and Sapolsky (1993) categorized the various types of violent acts occurring in their set of 30 films. They found an average of more than 50 aggressive acts per film. One in four assaults was judged to be "extreme"—stabbing resulting in a major injury or death, burning, dismemberment, beheading and bludgeoning. Clearly, slasher films provide viewers with a heavy dose of extreme brutality and sadistic victimization.

Trends in Slasher Violence. Have the complaints about the violent content and impact of slasher films led producers to alter the level of violence in such entertainment? Molitor and Sapolsky's study provides a glimpse at changing levels of victimization across three years: 1980, 1985 and 1989. When innocent victims of violence are considered, the number of violent acts against males increased across the three years; in contrast, injury and death decreased for females. Thus, across the decade males had to endure a greater share of the brutality as producers toned down their attacks against females.

Content analyses provide consistent evidence that females are *not* the predominant victims in slasher films. While attention has been paid to critics who have claimed that females are inordinately victimized, less attention has been given to those who focus on the female as survivor, hero and victor. Figurative analyses have examined the sex-gender system in slasher films; of particular relevance here is the "girl-victim-hero." Carol J. Clover [in her book *Men, Women, and Chainsaws: Gender in the Modern Horror Film,*] refers to the surviving female in slasher films as the "final girl":

> She is the one who encounters the mutilated bodies of her friends and perceives the full extent of the preceding horror and of her own peril; who is chased, cornered, wounded; whom we see scream, stagger, fall, rise and scream again. She is abject terror personified. . . . She alone looks death in the face, but she alone also finds the strength either to stay the killer long enough to be rescued . . . or to kill him herself. . . . But, in either case, from 1974 on, the survivor figure has been female.

The final girl has been overlooked in content analyses of slasher films. However, it is this female protagonist who may account for the significantly greater screen time during which females are shown in fear. For instance, in *The Texas Chainsaw Massacre* the final girl, Sally, endures prolonged terror: "For nearly thirty minutes of screen time—a third of the film—we watch her shriek, run, flinch, jump," [writes Clover]. We reanalyzed three of the films from the Molitor and Sapolsky (1993) study: *A Nightmare on Elm Street, Halloween 5* and *Friday the 13th VIII: Jason Takes Manhattan.* All three films feature a "final girl." The final girl accounted for two-thirds of the woman-in-terror screen time. Thus, it is quite possible that the portrayal of female characters in terror is largely attributable to the final girl's struggles with the killer, struggles in which the female ultimately triumphs. Analysis of a larger number of slasher films is needed to confirm this speculation. . . .

Concerns over Slasher Films Remain

The concern over potential negative effects of exposure to slasher films remains. Possibly, depictions of violence directed at women as well as the substantial amount of screen time in which women are shown in terror may reduce male viewers' anxiety.

Lowered anxiety reduce males' responses to subsequently viewed violence, including violence directed at women. Accordingly, the desensitizing effects of slasher films may result from a form of "extinction" and not from classical conditioning.

The heyday of slasher films has come and gone. Producers continue to search for new blends of death and mayhem to entertain and scare young audiences. It remains to be seen how far filmmakers will go to achieve these effects, and how audiences will react to what will no doubt be new levels of explicitness, deviance, and gore.

2

EXAMINING POP CULTURE

Violence on Television

The First Outcry Against Television Violence

Francis Wheen

Throughout the 1950s, television's first decade, westerns were by far the most popular genre for TV adventure. In the 1960s, crime dramas began to dominate network schedules, and shows featuring police and private investigators remain a staple of TV programming today. In this excerpt from his book *Television: A History*, Francis Wheen, a columnist for British newspaper the *Guardian*, notes that as early as 1959, with ABC's Prohibition-era drama *The Untouchables*, crime series drew criticism for their violent content. The first outcry against TV violence culminated in 1961, when Federal Communications Commission chairman Newton Minow called TV a "vast wasteland" and intimated that the FCC might intervene to monitor television content. Since then, TV violence has come in cycles, with the major networks periodically toning down their violent programming when public opinion demands it. Writing in 1985, Wheen notes that violent police shows dominated television in the 1970s, but that the trend seemed to be turning against violence in the early 1980s.

WHEN THE APPETITE FOR WESTERNS STARTED to diminish, in the 1960s, the networks and film companies had a simple solution: they increased production of that even

■

more enduring cornerstone of popular television drama—the crime series. In the 1960s and 1970s crime drama achieved the same kind of dominance which had been enjoyed by Westerns in the late 1950s, but even in the earliest years of American television it had been a regular feature on the schedules. The first episodic series of this sort was *Man Against Crime*, begun by CBS in 1949, which starred Ralph Bellamy as special investigator Mike Barnett. Writers on the series were instructed that 'somebody must be murdered, preferably early, with the threat of more violence to come.' Bellamy himself 'must be menaced early and often.'

The First Crime Dramas

For the first three years of its existence, *Man Against Crime* was transmitted live from CBS's studios at Grand Central Station in New York. To ensure that the programme ran to time, writers were instructed to include a 'search scene' near the end of each episode, in which Bellamy would hunt for a crucial clue. His search could be shortened or extended almost indefinitely when the show was on the air, so that it always finished punctually.

In 1952 *Man Against Crime* abandoned live production; episodes were filmed in advance instead. This may have been caused by the appearance of a rival action drama, *Dragnet*, which had been on film since its inception in December 1951 on NBC. *Dragnet* was created by Jack Webb, who also starred in the show as Detective Sergeant Joe Friday of the Los Angeles Police Department (the series was supposed to be based on the Department's actual case histories). Friday was not a character who wasted his words. 'My name's Friday—I'm a cop' was his usual way of introducing himself. One of his regular catchphrases was a plea for 'just the facts, ma'am.' *Dragnet* was immensely popular, running for 300 episodes between 1951 and 1958 and another 98 when it was revived in 1967. It was also the first American drama series to be sold to British television.

Film companies were not yet cooperating with television when *Dragnet* began, but the Hollywood settings were a foretaste of what was to come when agreement was reached with the networks three years later. By 1957 film studios were churning out crime series with almost as much enthusiasm as they were devoting to Westerns. The two genres were not all that dissimilar: both presented a simple, Manichean view of the world, whether it was divided into cops and crooks or cowboys and Indians. Out they poured—*Racket Squad, Official Detective, Suspicion, M Squad* and countless others. Even Broderick Crawford, who played a traffic policeman in *Highway Patrol*, managed to fit in plenty of crime-fighting between his admonishments about road safety and his introduction to the jargon of police radio ('Ten Four—and out'). *Naked City* was filmed in the streets of New York, and included ordinary passers-by as extras.

Endless Variations on the Theme

Over the next twenty-five years, producers of crime series tried just about every conceivable variation on a rather limited theme. The hero had to be given some quirk which would distinguish him from the heroes of every other action drama. There were blind investigators (*Longstreet*), overweight investigators (*Cannon*), scruffy, working-class investigators (*Columbo*), suave millionaire investigators (Amos Burke in *Burke's Law*), bald investigators who sucked lollipops and said 'Who loves ya, baby?' (*Kojak*), one female investigator (*Police Woman*), a pair of female investigators (*Cagney and Lacey*), three female investigators (*Charlie's Angels*), an ex-criminal turned investigator (*The Rockford Files*), a Vietnam veteran turned investigator (*Magnum PI*), a cowboy on assignment as an investigator in New York (*McCloud*), investigators in an exotic setting (*Hawaii Five-O*), buddy-buddy investigators (*Starsky and Hutch*)—the list could be extended indefinitely. In 1967 NBC introduced an investigator confined to a wheelchair, in *Ironside*. No gay investigators have turned up yet, but they will.

The hero of a crime drama did not have to be a police officer or a private detective. He could be a lawyer, as Raymond Burr demonstrated in *Perry Mason*, a courtroom drama which ran for eight years from 1957, in which Perry Mason invariably got the better of District Attorney Hamilton Burger. There was also a number of medical dramas which attracted high ratings; as network executives cheerfully explain, the dramatic potential of doctors is almost as great as that of the police, since they are constantly involved in life-or-death crises.

One distinctly above-average series in which lawyers were

Most People Watch Television Most of the Time

Everything network television is criticized for is, perversely, its strength. Mindless repetition, incessant cloning of the same genres and even the same shows, mediocre acting, short segments, fast action, endless commercial interruptions, abrupt cutting, and flashing imagery, overloud sound, predictable action, laugh tracks, reruns, mutilation of movies such as cutting and colorizing, superficiality—all these and more should alert us to this paradox. As terrible as the critics say it is, television is watched. . . .

Any study of television must begin with the recognition that in our culture most people watch it most of the time. After sleeping and working, watching video images is our favorite way to pass time. Well over ninety-five percent of American households have at least one television set, and the experience of watching has become the social and intellectual matrix which holds us together. Television *is* our culture. "Did you see . . . ?" has replaced "Do you know . . . ?," "Did you read . . . ?," or "Have you heard . . . ?" Television displays most of what we know and much of what we believe. . . .

When we move beyond specific content and look at the type of program that succeeds in finding the largest audience, we learn that of the five categories Nielsen uses (sitcoms, movies, adventure stories, general drama, mystery/suspense), the most-watched are, first, adventure stories and, second, movies. Movies have tended toward imaging action over character, and hence adventure, usually violent adventure, has prevailed. The very concept of adventure, of a hero going and doing something exciting, almost demands violence.

James B. Twitchell, *Preposterous Violence: Fables of Aggression in Modern Culture*, 1989.

the heroes was *The Defenders*, which was created for CBS in 1961 by Reginald Rose (author of *Twelve Angry Men*). It featured a father-and-son team of attorneys, played by E.G. Marshall and Robert Reed, who took up important but delicate issues such as abortion, black-listing and capital punishment. Herbert Brodkin, who produced the series, says that his intention was 'to do an entertaining series about the reality of life in New York from the real point of view . . . I think we were able to tackle some difficult subjects and do them quite well. We had marvellous writers, we had marvellous directors and we had New York actors. And we didn't have anyone to tell us that what we were doing was incorrect or wrong.' It lasted for 132 episodes, ending in 1965. '*The Defenders* almost changed the face of television,' Brodkin says. 'It was then that something called *Beverly Hillbillies* came along, and some others like it, and that changed it right back.' The networks gratefully retreated from the dangerous reality of *The Defenders* to their preferred diet of cop shows, which were to become increasingly violent.

'You've Got to Escalate the Violence'

But violence has its problems. 'The problem is,' says Les Brown, former TV critic of the *New York Times*, 'that the audience gets very sophisticated about these things, and it's a short order. If you've done violence and you've done quite a lot of it in the course of a week, then the audience doesn't find that very violent any more. You've already done that, so you've got to escalate the violence. You have to get more and more until the people start to scream—that is, decent people out there start to scream, and that's happened a few times. And then they come down hard on the networks and the producing companies.'

This first occurred in the early 1960s. Crime series had become more and more violent, reaching some kind of apogee with ABC's *The Untouchables*, first broadcast in 1959, which dealt with organised crime in the 1920s. It starred Robert Stack as the chief of the Federal Special Squad (nicknamed 'the untouchables' because of their incorruptibility during Prohibition). It is usually described as the most violent series ever shown on television. '*The Untouchables* was supposed to be violent, damn it,' the show's producer, Quinn Martin, once snapped. It won a large audience, but it also attracted the attention of those people who were becoming concerned about violence on the screen. A group in Los Angeles which monitored prime-time television in November 1960 found that in one week the networks had transmitted 144 murders, 143 attempted murders, 52 justifiable killings, 14 druggings, 12 jailbreaks, 36 robberies, 6 thefts, 13 kidnappings, 6 burglaries, 7 cases of torture, 6 cases of extortion, 5 cases of blackmail, 11 planned murders, 4 attempted lynchings, a massacre in which hundreds of people were killed, another mass murder and three shoot-outs between gangs. When Newton Minow was appointed by President Kennedy in 1961 to chair the Federal Communications Commission, he told the National Association of Broadcasters that he considered American television to be 'a vast wasteland' in which could be found 'game shows, violence, audience participation shows, formula comedies about totally unbelievable families, blood and thunder, mayhem, violence, sadism, murder, western bad-men, western good-men, private eyes, gangsters, more violence and cartoons. . . . Gentlemen, your trust accounting with your beneficiaries is overdue. Never have so few owed so much to so many.' Minow added a stinging *coda*: 'I understand that many people feel that in the past licences were often renewed *pro forma* [as a matter of form; that is, without scrutiny]. I say to you now, renewal will not be *pro forma* in the future.' The networks were so alarmed by Minow's threat that they cleaned up their acts—but not for long. Once the hue and cry had died down they returned to their old ways, which included the 'escalation of violence' as described by Les Brown. Senator Thomas Dodd held public hearings into television violence in 1961; he began as an implacable foe of the networks, but he suddenly performed an abrupt about-turn on the subject, and ordered that his report should not be published. It was later revealed that he had accepted lavish gifts from a number of television companies.

Half-Hearted Reforms

Every so often since then, the networks have temporarily 'toned down' the action in their shows when there has been an unusually loud public clamour about the effects of violence on television—after the assassination of President Kennedy in 1963, for instance, and after the deaths of Martin Luther King and Bobby Kennedy in 1968. When Bobby Kennedy was shot, several hundred leading actors and scriptwriters took advertisements in a number of papers, announcing that 'we will no longer lend our talents in any way to add to the creation of a climate for murder.'

But the television companies' public promise to reduce the level of violence in their dramas was never more than half-hearted. 'Please murder the baby tastefully' and 'Please see that the lady is raped without offending accepted decorum' were two (genuine) continuity notes given by networks to their producers in the 1970s. To appease the anti-violence groups who kept a tally of the number of murders in crime series, a few statistical adjustments were made: if a script called for ten people to be shot in a particular episode, the producer might reduce the number to two. By way of compensation for the smaller amount of physical action (punch-ups, shoot-outs and so on), producers increased the prevalence of what one might call 'mechanical violence'—explosive car chases accompanied by an exaggerated soundtrack of screeching tyres, which were *de rigueur* in the movies after *Bullitt* and *The French Connection*, also became a permanent feature of cop shows such as *Starsky and Hutch*.

There was a continuing and unresolved debate about how much influence televised violence really had on the minds of the viewers. Sometimes newspapers would seize on a case in which a youngster explained that he had committed a murder after seeing it done on television. But others dispute that television has that much effect, including some criminals themselves. 'If I'm going to rob a bank, there's going to be violence,' says David Peterson, who has been in San Quentin jail for the past ten years, having been convicted of first-degree murder. 'But I don't need television to rob a bank. If I'm going to go and rob a bank, I'm going to rob it. I ain't going to sit and wait for a television picture to come and see how they do it. I'm going to use my own ideas and go. I don't think violence on TV has done anything really to push violence.'

Hints of Progress

At the end of the 1970s, in fact, the violent cop shows did begin to disappear—not so much because of the work of pressure groups as because networks felt they had exhausted the seam. They also discovered that it was possible to achieve high ratings without festooning the script with multiple killings or car smashes. The most successful police series of the early 1980s was *Hill Street Blues*, a witty and amiable show set in a police station with a 'heavy ethnic mix.' Its first series, in 1980, was notable for eschewing the action stunts which had hitherto been thought essential. It won the record number of nine Emmy awards. In later series of *Hill Street Blues*, the car crashes began to creep back in, but the programme was still distinguished from its predecessors by its 'natural' filming style (hand held cameras, unsynchronised dialogue) and by the fact that its characters were presented as credible human beings. It was a far cry from *Charlie's Angels* or *Starsky and Hutch*.

Public Opinion on Television Violence

George Comstock and Erica Scharrer

Public concern over violence on television has shifted slightly over the years, but in general, since the 1950s about two-thirds of Americans have agreed with the statement that there is "too much violence" on television. However, when people are simply asked if they have seen something on television that offends them, less than 10 percent cite a violent portrayal. Similarly, very few people cite media violence as one of the most important problems facing the nation. The low priority the public gives the issue may explain why the broadcast industry has not instituted dramatic reforms in response to the periodic outcries against violence on television.

George Comstock is a professor of public communications at Syracuse University, and the author, with research assistant Erica Scharrer, of *Television: What's On, Who's Watching, and What It Means*, from which this article is excerpted.

THE FIRST CONGRESSIONAL HEARING DEVOTED to television programming was held in the House in 1952. The topics were violence and sex. The committee concluded that some programming was offensive, portrayals of crime and violence were excessive, and self-regulation was preferable to government intervention, but that Congress had prerogatives

■

despite the First Amendment because of the great potential for harm. This established the framework for numerous House and Senate hearings focusing on violence, and sometimes also sex, that would follow. These included very high profile hearings chaired by Senators Kefauver (1950s), Dodd (1960s), Pastore (1970s), and Simon (1990s).

Five federal fact-finding task forces have been concerned with media effects. The National Commission on the Causes and Prevention of Violence (1969), primarily concerned with rioting in urban Black communities, issued a compendium of research findings on the influence of media violence (Baker & Ball, 1969) and in its report specifically concluded that media violence contributed to antisocial behavior. The Commission on Obscenity and Pornography (1970) concluded that erotic media had no deleterious effects on antisocial behavior. The Surgeon General's Scientific Advisory Committee on Television and Social Behavior (1972), the sole inquiry primarily concerned with television violence, concluded that viewing violent programming increased the aggressive and antisocial behavior of some young viewers. The "Surgeon General's Update," a collection of commissioned papers and an overview by a committee of experts on the 10th anniversary of the report of the original committee, concluded that the evidence of the preceding decade strongly reinforced the initial conclusion. The Attorney General's Commission on Pornography (1986) concluded that media that portrayed females in a degrading manner or as the targets of violent assault, especially in a sexual context, increased aggressive and antisocial behavior on the part of males against females. Thus, four of the five endeavors concluded that violent media could be problematic in regard to the behavior of viewers, with one focused specifically on television entertainment.

Polls and Surveys on Media Violence

These institutional expressions of concern have had their counterpart in public opinion as measured by polls and surveys. The more prominent have been conducted by professional research organizations (Roper Starch, Gallup, Yankelovich, and others, often with media sponsorship) using national probability samples of about 1200 to 2000, so that outcomes can be said to accurately represent the American public.

Typically, about two-thirds of Americans have agreed (rather than disagreed or confessed to no opinion) with the statement that there is "too much violence" on television, although figures as low as 50% have been recorded. Such proportions have been highly stable since the 1960s.

The proportion agreeing with the statement that television violence is harmful or encourages crime and delinquency typically has been about three-fourths of that endorsing the view that there is too much violence. If 66% agree there is too much violence, about 50% will agree it is harmful.

The pattern for "sex" on television—or, more accurately, the intimation, description, or designation of sexual activity, since graphic intercourse is not a part of entertainment on broadcast or most cable channels—has been similar, except that it typically scores a very few percentage points behind violence in regard to "too much" or harmfulness. Violence and sex compete, along with the number of commercials, as attributes of television with which the public says it is most dissatisfied.

The public is sensitive to the degree of attention given to television violence by the media. With the congressional and presidential pressure of the 1990s and consequent media attention, the proportion agreeing there is too much violence has increased to about 80%. Poll after poll in the mid-1990s has reported comparable results.

This suggests a scenario in which public anxiety has been reflected in the response of politicians and public institutions. However, a closer look at the evidence reveals a very different picture.

Volunteered vs. Elicited Responses

In the late 1970s and early 1980s, the Reverends Jerry Falwell and Daniel Wildmon attempted to organize viewer boycotts in protest of television sex and violence and had singled out 16 programs as particularly offensive. When a nationally representative sample was asked without any reference to violence to name things disliked about these programs, the average citing violence was under 5%. During the same period, the percentage in comparable samples agreeing there was too much violence on television ranged from 50 to 66%.

The phenomenon is repeated in very recently [1995] published data by Roper Starch. When asked if they had seen something on television that offended them, only about 7% of a representative national sample cited a violent portrayal. This contrasts with the approximately 80% who during the same period endorsed the view that there is too much violence on television.

This is an example of a common circumstance—the radically different impressions about public views that may occur for "volunteered" opinions vs "elicited" responses. The former represent the free expression of views in response to a topic or subject area. The latter tabulate the selection of an option (agree, disagree, no opinion) in response to a preformulated stance. The more that volunteered opinions lag behind elicited responses in frequency, the less salient and deeply held is the opinion represented by the elicited responses, for the former represent viewpoints people are ready to articulate whereas the latter are merely multiple-choice endorsements.

The pattern has been repeatedly supported since World War II by the replies of the public when regularly asked by Gallup to name the most important problem facing the nation. Only a scant few have named media violence, even at times when the behavior of the media has been fairly high among the topics receiving attention in the news.

Overall, the data led us to four conclusions:

1. Television violence, along with other media issues, is of very low salience to the public. It is not a topic where opinion is heartfelt or concern is of high priority.

2. The widely published survey data have exaggerated the degree of public concern because of the mode of collection. Similarly, the high percentages currently being recorded for elicited opinion decline to their former levels when media attention declines.

3. The notion that politicians and the federal task forces have responded to public anxiety is incorrect. The low salience attached by the public to media issues suggest they are of concern primarily to elites—those who work in the media and in public life. The rise in the proportion expressing dissatisfaction with television violence is a consequence of the attention of public figures and the media rather than the reverse.

4. When attacked about some genre of content, the best defense of the media is to direct attention toward specific offerings. Our example has been television violence, but we believe the principle holds broadly. The public is ready to endorse harsh views about a medium in general, but is far less prepared to do so in regard to explicitly identified examples.

Measuring the Amount of Violence on Television

Barrie Gunter and Jackie Harrison

Researchers who study media violence use a method
known as content analysis to measure the "amount"
of violence different programs contain. Barrie Gunter
and Jackie Harrison, both professors in the department of journalism studies at England's University of
Sheffield, summarize the two largest content analyses
that have been conducted on television violence. The
first is the Cultural Indicators Project, which monitored violence in prime-time television from the late
1960s to mid-1980s. The second is the National
Television Violence Study, a three-year study begun
in 1994 that measured the amount of violence on
both cable and network programs.

TRADITIONALLY, THE MOST COMMONLY USED
method for assessing how much violence television programmes
contain is known as *content analysis*. When measuring violence
on television, researchers using content analysis begin by setting
up an 'objective' statement of what they mean by violence. Violence is defined in broad terms. Accompanying this definition
will be a frame of reference which specifies how and where that
definition should be applied in the assessment of programmes.
This instructional frame of reference is given to teams of trained
coders who watch samples of programmes recorded from television and count up incidents which match the definition of vi-

■

olence drawn up for the purposes of the analysis. This enables researchers to produce a quantitative assessment of the 'amount' of violence on television in terms of the numbers of violent incidents or events catalogued by coders.

Striving for Objectivity

Content analysis does not provide a measure of the effects of television violence, nor does it provide any sort of indication of public opinion about violence on television. Its aim is purely to yield an indication of the extent and location of particular classes of incident or event in television programmes. This research methodology attempts, as far as possible, to exclude any element of subjective judgement about violent television portrayals. All violence tends to be treated in the same way by a content analysis, regardless of the type of programme or dramatic context or setting in which it occurs. Thus, cartoon violence, for example, is treated no differently than violence occurring in a contemporary drama series. Traditionally, content analysis researchers define the intensity of violence in a programme in terms of the numbers of certain kinds of incidents it contains, rather than in terms of the nature of those incidents. This type of measurement does not, of course, reflect the way in which viewers might respond to violence on television. Research on viewers' perceptions of television violence has shown that viewers differentiate between violent portrayals on the basis of the context in which they occur, the form of violence displayed, and the types of characters involved as perpetrators or victims of violence. The important objective in content analysis, however, is consistency and reliability of assessment across different coders. It is essential that different coders should use the coding frame in the same way and produce the same or very similar incident counts, otherwise it would be impossible to obtain accurate measures of what has happened on television.

Even within the content analysis perspective, it is possible to utilize different definitional terms of reference. Content analysis methodologies can vary in terms of the definitions of violence they use, the way in which they sample programmes and the degree of detail they obtain about violence on television. Most content analysis, however, places emphasis on the specification of profiles and structures of programme content. With regard to the measurement of television violence, the commonality in the application of this technique lies in the objective counting of incidents which match a single normative definition of violence. . . .

The Cultural Indicators Project

The most extensive quantitative content analysis of television violence was carried out by Gerbner and his colleagues of the Annenberg School of Communications, University of Pennsylvania. This group analysed violence on network television in the United States over a period spanning nearly 20 years. Their primary focus was on prime-time evening television (7.30 pm to 11.00 pm) and Saturday and Sunday daytime television (8.00 am to 2.30 pm). The analysis was limited to dramatic entertainment programmes. News, documentaries, variety and quiz shows, and sports programmes were excluded. The samples taken annually for Gerbner's content analyses were typically single weeks of all dramatic fiction, including cartoons. In response to criticisms that one week was too small a sample, seven weeks were taken in 1976, yielding 409 programmes. By the mid-1980s, the data base apparently covered 2,105 programmes. After 1980, however, published analyses of the Violence Profile became more sporadic.

A single normative definition of violence was used: 'the overt expression of physical force (with or without a weapon) against self or other, compelling action against one's will on pain of being hurt or killed, or actually hurting or killing'. Further specifications were made that the incidents must be plausible and credible; but that no idle threats should be included. However, violent accidents or natural catastrophes, whose inclusion in dramatic plots was reasoned by Gerbner to be technically non-accidental, were included. The violence definition emphasized incidents resulting in the infliction of injury or suffering, but largely ignored the context in which incidents occurred. Any events likely to cause or actually causing injury to a character on screen were catalogued and given equivalent weightings of intensity or seriousness whether they occurred in contemporary drama or animated cartoons.

Using the above scheme to guide them, a team of trained

coders was employed to record such features as the frequency and nature of violent acts, the perpetrators and victims of violence, and the temporal and spatial settings in which the acts occurred. From certain combinations of these measures, Gerbner derived the 'Violence Profile' which purported to represent an objective and meaningful indicator of the amount of violence portrayed in television drama. . . .

The Violence Index

The amount of violence occurring on television was represented by the Violence Index. Essentially this index represented the percentage of programmes containing any violence at all, the frequency and rate of violent episodes per programme and per hour, and the number of leading characters involved in violence either as aggressors or as victims. . . .

Throughout the 1970s, Gerbner *et al.* monitored levels of violence in prime-time television drama programming in the USA. This work began in the 1967–68 television season. During the next ten years, an average of 80% of programmes contained violence and 60% of major characters were involved in violence. The average rate of violent episodes was seven and a half per hour, and in weekend, daytime children's programmes, violent episodes averaged almost 18 per hour. Indeed, programmes directed at children typically scored high on most measures of violence except for killing; cartoons in particular consistently exceeded all other categories of programmes, including adult action-adventure and crime-detective shows.

The overall rates of violence found by Gerbner *et al.* remained very consistent over the years, averaging five or six acts of overt physical violence per hour on prime-time television. The rates of violence per programme averaged 4.81 acts for prime-time television and 5.77 per programme for weekend daytime television. . . .

The Cultural Indicators project continued into the 1980s and revealed that the world of American network television was characterized more by stability than change. Despite year-on-year fluctuations in levels of violence, the general patterns of involvement in violence among different social groups were very consistent across a 20-year period. The index of violence reached its highest level since 1967, when the study began, in the 1984/85 television season. Eight out of every ten prime-time programmes contained violence at that time, and the rate of violence was nearly eight incidents per hour. The 19-year average was six per hour. Children's programmes were customarily found to be saturated with violence on American television. During the 1984/85 season, the average rate of occurrence was 27 violent acts per hour, compared with the 19-year average of 21 acts per hour for children's programmes....

The National Television Violence Study

The latest and most substantial American study of violence on television is the National Television Violence Study funded over three years (1994–97) by the national Cable Television Association in the United States. This study developed an elaborate methodology which assessed not just the quantity of violence depicted on American television, but also the nature of violent portrayals and context within which violence occurred.

The National Television Violence Study developed a definition of violence which embodied three concepts: the notion of credible threat of violence, the overt occurrence of violent behaviour, and the harmful consequences of unseen violence. The idea of credible threat covered situations where an individual threatened another in such a way that there was a realistic likelihood that violence would follow, with the perpetrator having the clear means to carry out such action. The harmful consequences of unseen violence covered scenes where someone is depicted suffering some kind of pain or discomfort, and indeed actual physical damage may be shown, and where other clues from the storyline establish that they were a victim of violence.

Studying the Context of Violence

Much emphasis was placed on the context in which violence occurred and an elaborate framework of analysis was created to enable a comprehensive classification of violence in terms of a range of attributes: its dramatic setting, motivational context, graphicness, rewards and punishments, severity of consequences for victims, physical form, and the nature of the perpetrators and victims. All these factors were rationalized in terms of their significance as possible mediators of audience response to media depictions of violence as signalled by the published research literature on media violence effects.

To underpin the emphasis on context the units of analysis adopted by this study were not restricted to the simple counting of individual acts of violence, as in previous studies of this sort. Three levels of measurement were devised: (1) the PAT; (2) the scene; and (3) the programme. A PAT represented an interaction between a perpetrator (P), an act (A), and a target (T). A sequence of PATs, either continuous and uninterrupted or separated by brief cutaways or scene changes, might comprise a violent scene and afforded an opportunity to examine relationships between discrete acts. Finally, the researchers here argued that larger meanings could be conveyed by the pattern of violence considered as a whole within a programme, which could only be effectively interpreted when analysed along with the context in which it was presented in the programme.

This study analysed a far larger sample of programme output than any previous American content analysis of televised violence. In total, the project sampled nearly 2,500 hours of material. The sample was not restricted to peak-time, unlike most earlier work. Furthermore, it used a random sampling frame to select programmes for analysis over a period of 20 weeks on 23 separate television channels. This provided for a more representative sampling of television output than the convenience sampling methods used by earlier published studies.

Relevant Findings

The first year of this study found a total of more than 18,000 violent interactions in the sample of programming monitored. Violence occurred in a majority (57%) of these programmes. Two-thirds of these incidents (66%) involved a perpetrator committing an actual behavioural act of violence. Far fewer interactions involved credible threats (29%) where the perpetrator demonstrated a clear intent to physically harm the target with the means to do so, and a small proportion of incidents (3%) involved depictions of the harmful consequences of unseen violence.

Violent programmes were found to vary quite a bit in terms of the number of violent interactions they contained.

The frequency of violent interactions per programme ranged from one to 88. Most of the programmes, however, clustered at the lower end of the frequency distribution, with 15% of programmes containing only one violent interaction, 12% containing two, and 10% containing three. This meant that slightly more than one-third of all violent programmes contained between one and three violent interactions. Another one-third contained between five and eight violent interactions, and the remaining one-third featured nine or more violent interactions.

The prevalence of violence varied significantly by programme genre. A higher percentage of movies and drama series contained violence compared to the overall average of television, whereas fewer comedy series, reality-based shows, and music videos contained violence. Perpetrators of violence were far more likely to be male than female, and in the majority of cases were individuals working on their own rather than in a group. Most violent characters were human, although over one in five were anthropomorphized animals or supernatural creatures. Perpetrators were mostly young to middle-aged adults; very few perpetrators of violence on television were children, teenagers or elderly people. Most perpetrators were white, with relatively few being members of any other particular ethnic group. The victim profile was very similar to the perpetrator profile.

In the case of four out of ten violent incidents, perpetrators used parts of their own body to hit, punch or kick their target. When weapons were used, hand held firearms were the most common. The next most common weapon type involved the use of unconventional instruments of aggression such as ropes or chairs. Violence was extremely graphic in its portrayal on relatively rare occasions. Nearly half of all incidents of violence were classified as occurring in purely fantasy settings, while more than four in ten were classed as fictional. Few incidents were regarded as real. Violent incidents were slightly more likely to be punished than rewarded. In about three in ten cases, violence was accompanied by self-condemnation by the perpetrator, or was criticized or punished by another person or by some form of authority, while self or other punishment followed in around four in ten cases. Immediate punishment for violence, however, was not common. In well over four in ten cases, no physical injury followed violence, and more than one in three incidents depicted unrealistic harm. On balance, violence on American television in 1994–95 was found to be largely sanitized. It was rarely punished immediately and rarely caused observable harm to victims.

Examining How Violence Is Presented on Television

S. Robert Lichter, Linda S. Lichter, and
Stanley Rothman

S. Robert Lichter, Linda S. Lichter, and Stanley
Rothman are the authors of *Prime Time: How TV
Portrays American Culture*, from which this article is
excerpted. The selection below deals with their study
of the first month of the 1992–1993 prime-time television season, in which the authors monitored every
character and socially relevant theme that appeared
on the four major broadcast networks.

In addition to simply counting the number of
shows or scenes that featured violence, the Lichters
and Rothman discuss the types of violence that were
shown and the context in which they were presented.
They note, for example, that many police dramas
were using more intense scenes of violence less often.
In addition, in prime time more "good guy" than
"bad guy" characters used violence, and this violence
was rarely condemned. Finally, the authors provide
some evidence—such as the prevalence of violent images in advertisements for TV shows—that the television industry markets violent fare more heavily than
other types of programming.

■

IN THE CURRENT DEBATE OVER TELEVISION VIO-
lence, perhaps the most incongruous comment came from CBS
president Howard Stringer. Arguing against overly restrictive
standards, he warned, "We don't want to turn the vast wasteland into a dull wasteland." Never mind the apparent admis-
sion that television is indeed a wasteland, or the inference that
its aridity is relieved by the flow of blood. Stringer should have
checked the full text of the famous speech by former FCC
Chairman Newton Minow. He called television "a vast wasteland . . . of blood and thunder, mayhem, violence, sadism, murder. . . ." Minow, that is, termed television a vast wasteland
partly *because* of the violence that critics were already con-
demning over thirty years ago, when he delivered his speech to
a startled audience of network executives.

The Backlash Against Television Violence

Stringer's infelicitous simile reflects the entertainment industry's aggrieved response to the most recent wave of public revulsion and government pressure against media violence. The
networks were forced to broadcast parental advisories as a result of numerous congressional calls for more stringent measures. The proposals range from a government-mandated rating system to a computer chip that would allow television
owners to prevent their sets from broadcasting violent shows.

All this legislative activity was spurred by an unusually
broad social consensus for reform. Polls show not only that
three-quarters of the public find TV entertainment too violent, but that an even higher percentage of TV station man-
agers agree. When asked to select measures that would reduce
violent crime "a lot," the public chose restrictions on TV violence more frequently than gun control. More ominously for
the industry, a majority of Americans believe that the federal
government should regulate the amount of violence on television. That polling result appeared less than two weeks after
Dick Wolf, a veteran producer of action-adventure shows, told
a trade magazine that "nobody wants [antiviolence] legislation
except the lunatic fringe."

Network programmers and producers reply that they are
being treated as scapegoats for public frustration over real-
world crime and violence. Among other things, they argue

that prime-time series are less violent than in the past, and that the broadcast network offerings are tame compared to what is available on cable. Our research shows that there is some truth in this, but that the argument is also somewhat misleading and self-serving.

Prime-Time Network Television Is Less Violent

First, it is true that cable fare is far more violent than broadcast programming. In a separate study that examined such major cable channels as USA, HBO, MTV, and Ted Turner's WTBS "SuperStation," we found that the average amount of violence on any *one* cable outlet roughly equalled that on ABC, CBS, and NBC combined. Ironically, though, much of the cable violence appeared on shows that had originally aired on the broadcast networks. It is hardly reassuring to learn that the networks' action-adventure shows just move to new outlets when they can no longer generate the huge audiences necessary to keep them on the prime-time schedule. At least, it is difficult to give the broadcast networks *moral* credit for discarding such shows once they are no longer profitable.

Second, it is undoubtedly true that the current prime-time schedule lacks the kind of high-profile action-adventure fare of the previous decade, such as "The A-Team," "Miami Vice," and "Magnum, P.I." Dick Wolf notes dryly, "I unapologetically produced 'Miami Vice' in the 1980s. The national taste had no problem seeing Colombian drug dealers shot on a weekly basis. That show wouldn't be on today." Nonetheless, there is still plenty of violence to be found during prime time in places that undermine suggestions of industry restraint for any purposes other than purely commercial ones.

The Study

Our review of a month of prime-time fictional series episodes found over a thousand scenes involving violence—1,005 to be exact. (We tallied scenes rather than individual acts of violence so that the results would not be distorted by equating a flurry of punches in a single fight scene with a whole evening's worth of aggressive acts. Only intentional acts of physical force counted as violence.) There was little difference among the big three, as the amount of violence ranged only from 264 scenes on NBC to 292 on ABC, with CBS in the middle at 275. Fox was only programming five nights a week but still found time to feature 174 scenes of violence, which projects to 245 across seven nights.

Moreover, this tally probably understates the violent flavor of prime-time programs. Because our study was limited to fictional series, we missed reality shows such as "Cops," which Fox has always featured prominently. Nor was most of this material limited to tame or comic violence of the sort found in "Road Runner" cartoons or "Three Stooges" shorts. One out of five violent scenes (207) involved gunplay, and nearly half (423) included some kind of serious personal assault beyond mere slaps, punches, destruction of property, and the like.

Nor did our sample include a sweeps period, which traditionally includes more sexy and violent material. In fact, it was the gratuitous violence of the May 1993 sweeps that infuriated

The Importance of Context

Not all violent portrayals are equal with regard to the risk they might pose. . . .

Consider, for example, a documentary about gangs that contains scenes of violence in order to inform audiences about this societal problem. The overall message about violence in such a program is likely to be quite different from that of an action-adventure movie featuring a violent hero. The documentary actually may discourage aggression whereas the action-adventure movie may seem to glamorize it. A comparison of a film like *Schindler's List* about the Holocaust with a film like *The Terminator* illustrates this difference.

Such a contrast underscores the importance of considering the context within which violence is portrayed. Indeed, the television industry itself has long recognized that violence can have different meanings depending upon how it is presented within a program. Standards and practices

Congress and fueled the most recent reform efforts. The TV movies that the networks aired that month included such fare as "When Love Kills," "Gunsmoke: The Long Ride," and "Murder in the Heartland," a two-part docudrama on mass murderer Charles Starkweather. The actor who played Starkweather later complained that ABC cut his big sexual mutilation scene. This burst of violent programming followed directly on the heels of hearings in which industry figures had laid on expressions of good will and assurances of diminishing violence.

As these examples illustrate, many memorable or unusually graphic acts of violence are portrayed in one-time events such as miniseries, made-for-TV movies, or theatrical releases that eventually have prime-time showings. None of this material was included in our study. Even apart from these additional factors, our tally shows that weekly fictional series averaged between three and four scenes of violence per episode.

guidelines at the broadcast networks warn against showing "callousness or indifference to suffering," "scenes where children are victims," and "portrayals of the use of weapons or implements readily accessible" to children. Most of these programming guidelines focus on contextual cues and the different ways that violence can be portrayed.

The significance of context is highlighted not only by television industry guidelines, but also by academic research. Several major reviews of social science research demonstrate that certain depictions are more likely than others to pose risks for viewers. For example, Comstock and Paik (1991) examined much of the experimental literature and concluded that three dimensions of a portrayal are important in predicting whether a program is likely to facilitate aggression among viewers: 1) how efficacious or successful the violence is, 2) how normative or justified the violence appears, and 3) how pertinent the violence is to the viewer.

Center for Communication and Social Policy, *National Television Violence Study 2*, 1997.

Violence Is Concentrated in a Few Series

Averages can be deceiving, of course. . . . Over half the episodes had no violence at all. At the other end of the spectrum, the ten most violent series accounted for over 60 percent of all violence shown. About one-quarter of all series contained four-fifths of all violence. The single most violent series, CBS's "The Hat Squad," included over 10 percent of all fictional prime-time violence and over a third of the violence found on CBS's fall schedule. This old-fashioned cop show featured 111 scenes of violence, an average of twenty-eight per episode.

Serious violence was even more concentrated. Ten series accounted for over 70 percent of all murders, shootouts, sexual assaults, and so forth; twenty series accounted for over 90 percent. The leader in serious violence, ABC's "Young Indiana Jones Chronicles," averaged sixteen scenes per episode, nearly one-seventh of the entire prime-time total. To make it into the top ten, a series had to average nine violent scenes or four scenes involving serious violence per episode.

Many of the most violent shows could have been made with few alterations almost anytime in television's history. Whether cop shows or Westerns, in sci-fi and historical settings alike, these action shows use violence in much the same way that episodic television has used it for decades. It provides excitement, keeps the plot moving, and allows the good guys to be placed in jeopardy and then to vanquish the bad guys. Action-adventure entries as diverse as "Covington Cross" (swordplay among medieval knights), "Raven" (martial arts), and "Round Table" (a generic cop show) shared these characteristics with "Young Indiana Jones" and "The Hat Squad."

What is missing from such shows are the massive gun battles and extended chase sequences of a decade ago. The high-body-count SWAT teams and secret agents licensed to kill have given way to a new wave of cop shows that use less violence to greater effect. This developing genre includes such series in our sample as "Law and Order," "In the Heat of the Night," and "Reasonable Doubts," along with lesser known efforts like "Angel Street," "Bodies of Evidence," and "Likely Suspects." Among the more recent entries to attract attention and critical acclaim are "Homicide" and "NYPD Blue." New-wave cop shows often use an initial act of serious violence to set the plot in motion and then follow up with more limited violence in later scenes. They portray violence more realistically than do most other series. They are also more likely to show fear and suffering by the victims of violence and to explore the dramatic and emotional context of individual violent acts.

Violence Is Presented Differently than It Was in the Past

Consider the hottest new series of the 1993–94 season, Steven Bochco's controversial "NYPD Blue." This is not a particularly violent series as cop shows go. But Bochco intensifies the emotional impact of the violence that does occur, whether by mimicking the feel of a local newscast covering an active crime scene or by using the slow motion and fast-cutting techniques associated with film director Sam Peckinpah. The victims of violence clearly suffer pain and anguish, and cops and crooks alike show fear and confusion at the use of violence. For example, during one shootout Detective Kelly (the star) is so unnerved that he repeatedly misses the bad guy, who is so frightened that he drops his gun anyway.

Like other members of this new genre of cop shows, this series clearly intends to associate violence with fear and danger rather than adventure and machismo. Nonetheless, the gritty mise-en-scène and realistic conventions make the violence seem especially intense and exciting. This type of show separates the critics who want to minimize violence per se from those who single out gratuitous violence that is presented cavalierly or used as a dramatic crutch. In any case, the new-wave cop shows are the exception rather than the rule in the way that they portray violence.

Good Guys and Bad Guys

Our study examined not only the amount of violence but the dramatic context in which it occurs. After all, this is at least partly what separates Shakespearean swordplay from Schwartzenneger and Stallone. So each time violence occurred, we asked whether it was sanctioned and what lasting effects it produced. The results were not encouraging to those who worry about the point of TV violence as well as the prevalence. Across the entire prime-time schedule, acts of violence were committed by good guys more often than bad guys, and they were rarely condemned as illegal or morally wrong. To top it off, violence rarely produced physical damage or even caused characters to behave any differently afterward.

We counted 278 good guy characters who behaved violently toward another person, compared to 212 bad guys. So truth, justice, and the American way were defended by violence more often than they were threatened by it. Another sixty-eight violent characters combined positive and negative traits, along the lines of a Robin Hood clone in "Covington Cross" who stole from the rich and gave to the poor, but kept a tidy carrying charge. A plurality of perpetrators (369 characters) were not clearly identified as either heroes or villains. In percentage terms, 30 percent of those who committed violence were positive characters, only 23 percent were negative, 7 percent played morally mixed roles, and 40 percent were neutral characters without clear-cut virtues or vices. Many of these "neutral" characters were police who appeared in cop shows, chasing or subduing suspects.

Although relatively few acts of violence are committed by bad guys in prime-time series, even fewer are explicitly condemned. Of course, it is usually not defended either. Nine times out of ten, violence just happens. Whether it seems necessary or uncalled for in terms of the overall narrative, it is not commented upon to bring the message home to viewers. Specifically, no judgment was made about the use of violence 89 percent of the times it occurred during the month of prime time we studied. It was explicitly declared to be necessary or acceptable 2 percent of the time, precisely the percentage of cases that denounced the use of violence.

Violence Is Rarely Condemned

Thus, scripts actually condoned violence as frequently as they condemned it. But another 7 percent of violent acts were declared illegal, making 9 percent overall that were presented as somehow wrong. Even when gunplay or other serious violence took place, such behavior was presented as bad or unlawful only one time out of eight (12 percent), although verbal defenses of violence dropped to only 1 percent of these extreme cases.

It may seem less surprising that violence is so rarely deemed worthy of comment if we also note how rarely it has any discernible effect on its targets. Fewer than one-quarter of the acts of violence produced any physical injury. Fewer than one-third even caused the victims to alter their behavior in any way. The largest proportion, another one in three, produced no physical or behavioral change whatsoever. When violence is so infrequently presented as hurtful or dangerous, the rationale for denouncing it may seem less compelling.

However much moralists may deplore television's frequently nonjudgmental approach to violence, it might be argued that what the action-adventure audience wants is excitement, not ethical instruction. Moreover, trendsetters like "NYPD Blue" seem to be moving in the direction that the critics urge. For all their differences, however, the old-fashioned shoot-em-ups and the new-wave cop shows in our study had one thing in common besides their portrayal of violence: Most were gone by the end of the season. In fact, seven of the ten most violent series failed to last out the season, as did eight of the ten with the most serious violence. Among the latter, only one new series ("The Commish") and one holdover ("In the Heat of the Night") were still on the air in 1994.

Giving Violence the Hard Sell

The failure of so many violent series belies Hollywood's claims that it is only giving the public what it wants. Similarly, it undercuts the industry's assertion that calls for reform are coming at a time when the network schedules are less violent than they once were. The absence of conspicuously violent hit shows does not demonstrate the networks' unwillingness to offer such fare. It simply reflects the audience's rejection of the network offerings. . . .

Our study uncovered one other piece of evidence that Hollywood is giving violence the hard sell even though consumers don't seem in a mood to buy. The networks' intentions are revealed by the pitch they make for their programs, as well as by the programs themselves. And minute for minute, the most violent part of the prime-time schedule is not the programs themselves but the advertisements or "promos" that the networks use to attract viewers to upcoming programs. During the month that we viewed, there were actually more violent scenes in the promos for future programming fare than in the series episodes that were the subject matter of the rest of the study. The promos contained 1,313 violent scenes, compared to the 1,005 that we tallied during three hundred half-hour and hour-long programs.

The comparison isn't quite fair, because we counted promos for movies as well as series episodes, and it is movies that are most heavily promoted. For example, our study picked up thirteen airings of promos for the Steven Segal action flick "Under Siege," which totaled seventy-two scenes of violence. On the other hand, the promos themselves were extremely brief, typically lasting either fifteen or thirty seconds. Frequently inserted as teasers between the credits of the previous program and the start of the next one, they typically pulled together the most violent moments of a show in rat-tat-tat fashion, rather like armed NFL highlight films.

Ironically, these repeated doses of concentrated violence probably gave ammunition to critics by making the program schedule seem more violent than it actually was. The promos for some heavily promoted programs added nearly as much violence to prime time as the shows themselves contained, since they showed the same violent acts over and over again. So when programmers claim that they are just feeding the audience's taste for violent fare, it is well to remember how they choose to whet that appetite.

Video Games: The Latest Format for Screen Violence

Paul Keegan

Paul Keegan is a freelance writer whose work has appeared in a variety of national magazines. In the following excerpt from a feature he wrote for *Mother Jones*, Keegan describes controversy that arose over violent video games after the April 1999 school shooting in which two teenagers killed thirteen people at Columbine High School in Littleton, Colorado. Some critics blamed the shootings in part on violent games that the two killers had played. On the other side of the debate were the video game industry and gamers themselves, who claim that outcry against realistically violent games is misplaced.

Keegan visited the 1999 E3 convention—where the video game industry showcases its latest products—in order to experience the newest games for himself. Keegan also interviewed a group of avid gamers as well as several academics who have studied video games. He includes their views as well as his own as he questions whether video games will, like movies and television, become increasingly violent as the medium evolves.

WALKING DOWN FIGUEROA STREET TOWARD the Los Angeles Convention Center earlier this year [1999], it was impossible to miss the giant white face staring down from

■

a billboard, the eyes glowing bright yellow-orange, the pupils twisted into black spirals. The promotion for the Sega Dreamcast, a new video-game console, was designed to psych up game fans for the zoned-out bliss awaiting them at E3—the Electronic Entertainment Exposition trade show—then getting under way.

But because it appeared just three weeks after the school shootings in Littleton, at a time when video and computer games were emerging as a favorite target of blame, the image suddenly took on new meaning. It succinctly posed the biggest question surrounding the mammoth, $6.3 billion electronic-games industry, now poised to blow past Hollywood in terms of both annual revenue and cultural impact: What's going on behind those eyes?

The Video Game Violence Debate

Images of evil that are destroying our children's minds, cried the critics immediately after it was reported that Eric Harris and Dylan Klebold were avid players of the popular shoot-'em-ups Doom and Quake. CBS's "60 Minutes" broadcast a segment a few days later asking, "Are Video Games Turning Kids Into Killers?" Bills were introduced on Capitol Hill to ban the sale of violent video games to minors. In June, President Clinton ordered the surgeon general to study the effects of all violent media on children and young adults. He singled out video games in particular, pointing to research showing that half the electronic games a typical seventh-grader plays are violent. "What kind of values are we promoting," chimed in Hillary Clinton, "when a child can walk into a store and find video games where you win based on how many people you can kill or how many places you can blow up?"

The industry launched a counteroffensive, arguing that the vast majority of video games sold today are not violent, and emphasizing that no causal link has ever been established between aggressive behavior and prior exposure to violent media. "The entertainment software industry has no reason to run and hide," said Doug Lowenstein of the Interactive Digital Software Association (IDSA) at E3's opening press conference. He insisted that the simple reason the electronic-games industry is growing twice as fast as the movie business, and four times faster than the recording or book publishing industries, is that they "offer some of the most compelling, stimulating, and challenging entertainment available anywhere, in any form."

And so the E3 love-in carried on as usual this year, with 50,000 people jammed into an enormous exhibition space to sample the hottest new games. But as I wandered through the booths amid a constant roar of car crashes, monster screams, gunfire, and deafening techno-pop soundtracks, I wondered how this industry could have become so wildly popular in some circles and so utterly vilified in others. Is it true, as game developers like to say, that future generations will look back at today's controversy with the kind of bemusement now reserved for those grainy black-and-white images of crew-cutted right-wingers denouncing comic books and rock 'n' roll back in the 1950s? Or do critics have a point in saying that today's media technology has become so powerful and ubiquitous that a laissez-faire attitude toward pop culture is naive and outdated, if not outright dangerous?

Clues to the answers lie within a peculiar subculture of young, white, American males who make up the industry's technological vanguard. But to get a sense of what's behind those swirling eyeballs, first you have to play some games.

From Myst to Duke Nukem

According to industry ethos, the coolest electronic titles are not video games, which are played on dumbed-down console units made by Sony, Nintendo, and Sega, and account for nearly three-quarters of all game sales. Rather, the cutting edge is occupied by computer games—the other slice of the pie—because they run best on souped-up PCs that allow hardcore fans to customize a game by tinkering with its programming code.

Leaving the noisy main hall at E3, I enter a hushed room full of educational PC gaming titles and stop at the Mindscape Entertainment booth to check out the latest version of Myst, the best-selling PC title of all time. Myst earned its widespread popularity without benefit of rocket launchers or flying body parts. It's a role-playing game that takes place on a bucolic, forested island surrounded by clouds and ocean. The images are beautifully rendered: The forest mist is finely textured, and even the crevices on the tree bark are crisp and clear. The object of the game is to figure out why a team of scientists who were doing research on the island suddenly disappeared.

The game has a stately pace as you click through the foggy pathways and walkways, searching for clues. It's like looking at a series of pretty pictures. But if one thing is clear from spending time at E3, it's that this industry is driven largely by the pursuit of quite a different sensory experience: raw speed. That's true across the board, for the makers of PC games and video games alike. Sony, Nintendo, and Sega—all of which will introduce superpowerful, 128-bit game consoles to the market in the coming year—are not spending billions of dollars to create clever story lines. They are competing madly with one another to create the fastest video-game console ever, each boasting more horse-power than some of the most powerful supercomputers packed just 10 years ago. . . .

Myst is a storybook compared to the other games out in the main exhibition hall. There, I could lead a battalion of spaceships through the galaxy, make players dunk basketballs and hit home runs, and drive around a track in a race car. All of these games draw the player's attention because of that sense of moving through space; an appreciation of the rules and subtleties of gameplay come later.

But as thrilling as these games are, something's missing from all of them—something I can't quite put my finger on until I come upon an enormous poster of a guy who looks like an Aryan Nation thug: blond crew cut, open vest, a gun in each hand.

Duke Nukem is one of the bad-boy "first-person shooter" games that have brought such disrepute to the industry. Though shooters represent less than seven percent of overall sales, a recent Time/CNN poll showed that 50 percent of teenagers between 13 and 17 who have played video games have played them. Ten percent say they play regularly. A breakthrough game will fly off the shelves: Best-selling shooters Doom and Quake have had combined sales of 4.2 million. (Myst and its sequel, Riven, top the sales charts at 5.4 million.)

Real-Time 3-D Shooters

What makes these shooter games so compelling is the addition of freedom of movement to the sensation of speed. This is accomplished by the highly sophisticated underlying technology, called "real-time 3-D." Unlike the "pre-rendered" art of Myst—which limits your wanderings to predetermined paths—these images are not created in advance, but rather in "real time," on the fly, with the computer calculating at astronomical rates. Thus you get a euphoric sense of entering a fantastic new world and being able to roam about at breathtaking speeds. That freedom of movement is what's missing from the other games out on the floor at E3: The space game didn't let me go inside the ship, and the racing simulation wouldn't even let me get out of the car. Real-time 3-D gives you the illusion of maneuvering with no restrictions whatever.

Because real-time 3-D games and their fans stand firmly on the technology's leading edge, they represent a new avant-garde in popular entertainment—in much the same way that innovative independent films have an impact on Hollywood far beyond what their grosses might suggest. In both cases, tastes and techniques formed in one subculture eventually migrate to the broader culture, with enormous impact.

One of the most remarkable new titles is Quake III Arena, on display at the id Software booth. The Dallas-based company has perhaps the most advanced game software on the market. The detail in Quake III Arena is stunning—you believe you can reach out and touch the stone dungeon walls. Using the mouse, you can look around 360 degrees, which immediately makes you feel inside the gorgeous picture you're looking at. Able to go in any direction by pressing the arrow buttons on the keyboard, you instinctively start navigating this strange new universe, learning its laws of physics, mastering its peculiar rules and logic. When you jump from a launching pad located in outer space, it's exhilarating to hurtle through the airless void. This is virtual reality for the masses, on your home computer, without goggles or a trip to the arcade. . . .

But Quake III Arena, like all shooters, gives you only a few seconds to enjoy the medium before you get the message, loud and clear. As you drop hundreds of feet through space, you notice other inhabitants milling about on the landing platform below. Being a friendly sort, you approach them.

Big mistake: They open fire. Reflexively, fearfully, you begin to shoot back. Heads and arms start exploding.

In this magical environment, only one form of social exchange is permitted. The images this astonishing new technology is most often called upon to render so lovingly are rivers of blood and chunks of torn flesh.

"A Bunch of Kids Who Like to Play Games"

In a middle-class neighborhood in suburban Dallas, five young guys in their 20s sit on two long, black leather couches. It's an ordinary living room except that the couches do not face each other. They are side-by-side, facing the altar: a video screen big enough to be a clubhouse they could all climb into.

These guys—"a bunch of kids who like to play games," says Steve Gibson, a skinny 23-year-old with long sideburns, in his soft, slightly embarrassed voice—are living out the fantasy of every hardcore gamer: earning a living making and playing 3-D action games. Steve runs a gaming website called shugashack.com; the rest work at companies that have sprouted up here after the runaway success of id Software's Doom and Quake in the mid-'90s. As shooter fans, they belong to a largely hidden subculture whose members serve as the ultimate arbiters of cool within the larger electronic-games industry.

They go wild over shooter games not because they are inherently any more bloodthirsty than the average American male—they say they simply love the real-time 3-D programs and the sensations they stimulate. When it comes to "story," they care primarily about allowing the technology to fully express itself—which rules out peaceful adventure games like Myst that don't push the technological envelope or provide that crucial adrenaline rush.

Dan, Jack, Steve, Patrick, and Scott are nice guys—smart, courteous, some of them shy, others outgoing—and when they say that blowing away zillions of digital characters since they were kids hasn't made them the least bit aggressive in real life, you believe them.

"You're detached from the violence," explains Dan Hammans, a 19-year-old who, playing under the name Rix, has won several major Quake tournaments.

"Yeah, saying you like computer games for violence is like saying you like baseball for running," Jack adds. "Violence is there to grab people, get them into it, and have them say,

'That looks cool.' But once you get into it, you don't even notice the violence. You don't go, 'Oh, cool, he blew up!'"

Their comments remind me of Marshall McLuhan's theory that all technology has a certain numbing effect, which he compared with Narcissus' rapture at lake's edge. Though every medium has this narcotic effect, McLuhan argued, modern technology is progressing so fast that we can finally see these changes as if for the first time, "like a growing plant in an enormously accelerated movie."

The Link Between Video Violence and Aggression

McLuhan uttered his famous dictum—"The medium is the message"—at a time when television was the miraculous new medium, and social scientists focused on the message, which was violence. Today's media experts say the last four decades of research (including a 1972 surgeon general's report) have shown a clear correlation between violence on television and the development and display of aggressive values and behavior by both children and adults.

So there's a statistical correlation. But is there direct proof of cause and effect? "Not only isn't there proof, but there may never be proof," says Kansas State's John Murray [a professor and child psychologist]. But, he continues, "At some point, you have to say that if exposure to violence is related to aggressive attitudes and values, and if [the latter] are related to shooting classmates or acting aggressively—all of which we know to be true—then it stands to reason that there is probably a link between exposure to violence and aggressive actions.". . .

There hasn't been much research into the effects of video games, Murray says, and that's not only because they're so new. Many of the experts believe their point has already been proven, as much as humanly possible, with television. "It's a direct translation to video games," says Murray. "The only thing that's different and more worrisome is that the viewer or player is actively involved in constructing the violence."

According to other critics, playing games from the point of view of the killer is making some kids start thinking and acting like assassins. Lt. Col. Dave Grossman, a former West Point psychology professor, has been appearing on media outlets nationwide to plug his new book, *Stop Teaching Our Kids to Kill* (co-authored with Gloria DeGaetano), and to argue that children are getting the kind of sophisticated military training that until recently only the Pentagon could provide. "For the video game industry to claim that [research on] television and movie violence doesn't apply to them is like saying data on cigarettes doesn't apply to cigars," he says.

Most Gamers Are Not Violent

All these experts sound convincing until you find yourself in a Dallas living room chatting with five regular guys who play Quake long into the night, night after night. The fact that 99.99 percent of the kids who play violent games don't commit murder, they contend, disproves the experts' theories.

And in truth, not only do the games seem utterly harmless on this night, but these guys have so much fun playing together that it's hard to imagine the experience as anything but positive. Their camaraderie is as real as you'll find in any locker room. "It's how geeks get out their competitive spirit," says Steve, "because they're not athletic enough to play on the basketball team."

So benign is the mood here that I'm surprised by their reaction to a new game called Kingpin: Life of Crime. I fully expect them to draw the line here—for this is a game that goes way over the top with its graphic violence and racial stereotypes. Instead, they laugh and nod their approval at what a great game Kingpin is.

Kingpin takes place in a ghetto. As the game starts, you're lying in an alley, having been beaten up by a rival gang. You want revenge, but don't know who to trust. You need guns and money to survive, and quickly learn that the easiest way to do that is to kill people. . . .

Separating the medium from the message is not easy when it comes to technologically advanced games like Kingpin because the two are so deeply intertwined—its dreamlike, three-dimensional world will vanish unless you learn to kill.

An Increasing Tolerance for Violence

But regardless of whether you prefer McLuhan's theory about the numbing effect of the medium itself, or Murray's belief that desensitization flows from the constant message of mayhem, the result appears to be the same: a gradual increase in our cultural tolerance of violence, one we don't even notice until something shocking and new like Kingpin jolts us from our stupor.

Does that mean today's most gruesome games will eventually become so commonplace that they will elicit nothing more than a bored yawn? That's already happening among today's hardcore gamers, those taste makers who must give a computer game their blessing before it has much chance of migrating to the mainstream video-console market. Which makes hanging out with the Dallas shooter fans a bit like spending time in the future.

The main problem with Kingpin's story is not the violence or the stereotypes, they say, but that it's too self-conscious. "It burned me because it seems like they tried to be shocking," says Jack Mathews, a baby-faced 22-year-old programmer. "Like, 'Look, we're saying "fuck" all the time.' But frankly, the whole game industry is not a very mature industry."

His last comment may reveal the most crucial point: that spending long periods of time absorbed in any medium, especially one as immersive as a video game, can keep you locked safely in a bubble, protected from the real world, in an extended state of arrested development. Growth, after all, seldom occurs without pain. Is the recent rash of school shootings being caused, at least in part, by the exponential increase in technology's ability to numb pain by drawing kids into an isolated world where violence and aggression have no consequences?

Eugene Provenzo thinks so. The professor of education at the University of Miami, who is writing a book called *Children and Hyperreality: The Loss of the Real in Contemporary Childhood and Adolescence*, believes we're only at the beginning of an evolutionary process—one that has seen the gory comic book of the 1950s evolve first into the slasher movie and now into virtual nightmares like Kingpin. "I've been trying hard to make people realize we're going into a very different culture as a result of the introduction of new technologies," says Provenzo. "Video games are extremely powerful teaching machines, and we're still at a primitive level. We're on a trajectory toward increasing realism, or hyperreality, that makes people start thinking they can shoot someone and it doesn't hurt, that they can recover.". . .

Fantasy vs. Real Life

The computer-gamers gathered in the Dallas living room say they feel as though they don't hear enough about the evils of other media—which, they point out, are far more politically powerful and entrenched than the electronic-games industry. "When people see stuff [like Littleton] happen, they say, 'Oh, these computer freaks! Look at them, they're freaks!'" says Jack. "But when people see violence on TV, creatures exploding and people running around shooting with a shotgun, it's okay."

Dan acknowledges that what he loves about playing is that feeling of "being in another world with no consequences of your actions. You can jump off a ledge and smack on the ground and enjoy it." But there's a crystal-clear distinction in their minds between fantasy and real life, they add quickly, and for much of the evening they argue that spending so much time in their virtual worlds doesn't affect them at all. . . .

But how could it not? If media doesn't affect real-world behavior, there would be no such thing as advertising, which at last count was a $25 billion international business. Exactly how it affects us depends on the person, of course, and the effect can be quite subtle. But arguing that these games have no effect at all is absurd, given that everybody in this room is devoting his life to developing increasingly powerful ways of fooling your mind and body into believing the game experience is really happening to you.

I have one last question for these guys. Isn't there anything else they would like to do in their miraculous virtual worlds besides killing people and blowing things up?

"It's more fun to blow up things than to build things," explains Dan.

Jack shrugs. "Violence sells.". . .

A Crossroads in the Debate over Video Violence

The stakes are high, say social critics like Eugene Provenzo, who believes that our embrace of electronic games represents nothing less than a massive renegotiation with reality, with profound implications for how kids, in particular, learn about and understand the world. As supercomputers and expanding band-width change passive television into an interactive medium that can draw us into the most astonishing simulated worlds, we are nearing a crossroads at least as important as the moment flickering television images began transforming the American cultural landscape in the '50s.

It was decades before the effects of television were broadly debated—by which time screen violence was something kids simply took for granted as a normal part of childhood. We have the chance to do things differently this time, but it may require discussions more imaginative than the usual free-market versus government-control polemics. Entertainers from Snoop Doggy Dogg to network-cop-show producers have eased up on the brutality lately, and consumers seem more open to the possibility that today's mass media may be creating public health problems as severe as those caused by our disruption of the natural environment during the last great technological revolution.

But a question remains: Now that the shock of Littleton has subsided, will we simply return to a fantasy world where we can pretend that the ways we choose to entertain ourselves have no consequences, like some kid zoned out in front of a computer game? If so, game's over.

3

EXAMINING POP CULTURE

Research on Media Violence

The Effects of Media Violence

National Television Violence Study

In the early 1990s, public concern over violence on television intensified to such a degree that policymakers called on the entertainment industry to more closely examine the way in which violence is shown on television. In 1994 the National Television Violence Study (NTVS), a three-year research effort, was commissioned. The study involved researchers from four universities as well as the oversight of several national policy organizations.

In the section of the report excerpted below, the authors present an overview of the research that has been conducted on the effects of viewing media violence. The study concluded: 1) Heavy viewers of media violence exhibit increased aggression toward others, 2) prolonged exposure to media violence can lead to callous attitudes toward real-life violence, and 3) viewing media violence can lead to increased fears of real-life violence.

WE LIVE IN A VIOLENT SOCIETY. AS A NATION WE rank first among all developed countries in the world in homicides per capita. The pervasiveness of violence is alarming, particularly involving children and adolescents. What accounts for these trends? There is universal agreement that many factors contribute to violent behavior, such as gangs, drugs, guns, poverty, and racism. Violence is truly multifaceted, such that these factors may independently and interactively combine to

■

generate anti-social behavior. Viewing media violence is not the only, nor even the most important, contributor to violent behavior. Furthermore, it is not every act of violence in the media that raises concern, nor every child or adult who is affected. Yet there is clear evidence that exposure to media violence contributes in significant ways to violence in society. This conclusion is based on careful and critical readings of the social science research collected over the last 40 years.

During the past few decades many governmental and professional organizations have conducted exhaustive reviews of the scientific literature on the relationship between media violence and aggressive behavior. These investigations have consistently documented that media violence contributes to the aggressive behavior of many children, adolescents, and adults, as well as influencing people's perceptions and attitudes about violence.

Two early reports from the government's leading public health agencies, the 1972 Surgeon General's Report and the

Television Affects the Cultural Environment

"If you don't like what's on TV, just turn it off."

That solution has been offered like the trump card of reason in countless debates over the effects of the tube. But it's as useful as saying, "If you're troubled by air pollution, just stop breathing.". . .

In 1964, the Surgeon General's report on "Smoking and Health" confirmed that cigarette smoking causes lung cancer and contributes to heart disease. Now we know that the harm of smoking comes not only to those who choose to ignore the warning labels and light up, but also to a great many who never do. The costs associated with the public health crisis caused by tobacco are a burden we all share—even those of us who neither profit nor partake.

So too with popular culture that mainstreams degenerate and inhumane behavior. We can't simply switch it off

1982 National Institute of Mental Health [NIMH] review, concluded that television occupied a significant role in the lives of both children and adults. Both of these reports were emphatic in their claim that many types of televised violence can influence aggressive behavior. The Surgeon General's Report concluded there was a consistent and significant correlation between viewing televised violence and subsequent aggression. This finding emerged across many different measures of aggressive behavior and across different methodological approaches (e.g., experimental evidence, longitudinal field studies) to studying the problem. The Surgeon General's research made clear that there was a direct, causal link between exposure to televised violence and subsequent aggressive behavior by the viewer.

The NIMH report, which followed ten years later, added significantly to the conclusions of the Surgeon General. First, the age range of the effects was extended to include preschoolers and older adolescents, and the findings were generalized to girls as well as to boys. Secondly, and perhaps more important,

and live our lives as if it doesn't exist, because it changes our environment.

Thirty years ago, in the raw-nerved period following the murders of Martin Luther King Jr. and Robert Kennedy, President Johnson appointed a National Commission on the Causes and Prevention of Violence to review all the evidence and report on what the United States needed to do to reverse its downward course. Before 1968 came to an end, the American people were warned that television has the potential to foster moral and social values "which are unacceptable in a civilized society."

There were, naturally, those who disputed those findings—just as there were those who wouldn't accept the fact that cigarette smoking is dangerous. But there is one indisputable fact of life: When you ignore common sense, the chickens eventually come home to roost.

Mary Ann Watson, *Television Quarterly*, Spring 1999.

it was established that viewers learn more than aggressive behavior. They learn to fear being a victim. Heavy viewing may lead to aggression, but for some individuals it will lead to fear and apprehension about being victimized by aggression. It is more than aggressive behavior, the report concluded, that should be of concern.

In recent years additional reports, particularly from the Centers for Disease Control (1991), the National Academy of Science (1993), and the American Psychological Association (1993) have lent further support to the conclusion that the mass media contribute to aggressive attitudes and behavior. Perhaps the most comprehensive of these reports comes from the American Psychological Association, which concluded that:

> there is absolutely no doubt that those who are heavy viewers of this violence demonstrate increased acceptance of aggressive attitudes and increased aggressive behavior.

Such exposure is particularly problematic for children, who are just in the process of creating behavioral patterns that can have lifelong consequences.

Emotional Desensitization Toward Violence

In addition to increasing aggression toward others, viewing televised violence can significantly change attitudes and behaviors. Even those who do not themselves behave violently are affected by their viewing of violence in two important ways.

First, prolonged viewing of media violence can lead to emotional desensitization toward real world violence and the victims of violence. This in turn can result in callous attitudes toward violence directed at others and a decreased likelihood to take action on behalf of the victim when violence occurs. Research on desensitization to media violence has shown that although observers react initially with relatively intense physiological responses to scenes of violence, habituation can occur with prolonged or repeated exposure and this habituation can carry over to other settings. Once viewers are emotionally "comfortable" with violent content, they also may evaluate media violence more favorably in the future.

Second, viewing violence can increase the fear of becoming a victim of violence, with a related increase in self-protective behaviors and increased mistrust of others. Research by [George] Gerbner and his colleagues has shown that heavy viewers of media violence tend to have a perception of social reality which matches that presented in the media. That is, heavy viewers tend to see the world as more crime-ridden and dangerous, and are more fearful of walking alone in their own neighborhoods. Furthermore, viewing violence increases viewers' appetites for becoming involved in violence or exposing themselves to violence.

In summary, the research literature over the last three decades has been highly consistent in its findings in three major areas of effects of exposure to media violence. First, there is increased violence toward others due primarily to the effect of *learning and imitation*. Second, there is increased callousness toward violence among others, which has commonly been labeled the *desensitization* effect. And third, there is increased *fearfulness* (both in the short and long term) about becoming a victim of violence, often referred to as the "mean world syndrome" by Gerbner and his colleagues. Collectively, this evidence represents the scientific basis for concern about the effects of televised violence on the audience.

Questioning the Research on Media Violence

Jacob Sullum

Although many studies have examined the link between media violence and aggressive behavior, the
claim that violent entertainment causes real-life violence is a controversial one. Jacob Sullum, a senior
editor at *Reason* magazine, rebukes the notion that
there is a causal connection between fictional and
real-life violence. Much of the research on the issue
is flawed, he writes, and many studies only prove a
correlation between media violence and aggression. It
may be that aggressive people are simply more drawn
to violent entertainment, he notes. Sullum concludes
that politicians and the media have mischaracterized
and exaggerated the evidence against screen violence.

"THE VERDICT ON VIOLENT ENTERTAINMENT IS
now in," Senator Sam Brownback recently declared. "Violent
entertainment is a public health hazard."

To back up that claim, the Kansas Republican touted a
joint statement from the American Medical Association, the
American Psychological Association, the American Academy
of Pediatrics, and the American Academy of Child and Adolescent Psychiatry. "Well over 1,000 studies," it said, "point
overwhelmingly to a causal connection between media violence and aggressive behavior in some children."

To the average person, that sounds pretty impressive. But

■

From "Naughty Pictures," by Jacob Sullum, *Reason* Online, August 2, 2000.
Reprinted by permission of *Reason* Online. Copyright © 2001 by Reason Foundation,
3415 S. Sepulveda Blvd., Suite 400, Los Angeles, CA 90034, www.reason.com.

to anyone familiar with the research in this area, the statement is puzzling.

Jonathan Freedman, a University of Toronto psychologist who recently completed a review of the scientific literature, counts about 200 published studies that have tried to measure the impact of TV or film violence on aggression. "Anyone who says 'over 1,000' obviously has not looked at the research," he says. "It's so blatantly out of line."

Nor is it correct to say that the research "overwhelmingly" confirms the belief that watching fictional violence leads to violence in real life. "The majority of studies do not find evidence that supports the notion that television violence causes aggression," says Freedman.

Flawed Research

Most of the studies are laboratory experiments in which the viewing experience is very different from actual TV or movie watching and the "aggression" is far removed from the sort of violence that people worry about. In one famous experiment, for example, preschoolers who were shown a film of a man attacking an inflatable clown doll were more likely to knock the toy around than preschoolers who didn't see the film.

The relevance of such studies to real-life situations is questionable, to say the least. The problem is compounded by the fact that a researcher's expectations can influence a subject's behavior (as well as the way the behavior is evaluated).

"The showing of the violent film, which is usually a very short excerpt, almost inevitably carries a message that this is expected or allowed or wanted," Freedman observes. "It's very artificial research."

Field studies, in which the everyday behavior of subjects exposed to violent fare is compared to that of subjects who watch tamer stuff, attempt to address some of these weaknesses. But they produce inconsistent results, with only about 25 percent, by Freedman's estimate, providing support for the hypothesis that violent entertainment increases aggression.

Correlation Is Not Causation

Finally, there are correlational studies, which generally find that kids who watch more violent TV tend to be more aggres-

TV Encourages Good Behavior, Too

In a discerning op-ed piece in the *New York Times* author Patrick Cooke made [this] observation: If young Americans have seen tens of thousands of murders on TV, surely, he commented, they have seen even more acts of kindness. On sitcoms, romantic comedies, movies of the week, soaps, medical dramas, and even on police shows, people are constantly falling in love and helping each other out. The characters on most prime-time shows "share so much peace, tolerance and understanding that you might even call it gratuitous harmony," Cooke observes. Why not conclude, he asks, that TV encourages niceness at least as much as it encourages violence?

Yet social scientists who study relationships between TV violence and real-world violence, and whose research journalists, politicians, and activists cite in fear mongering about crime on TV, do not make niceness one of their outcome measures.

Barry Glassner, *The Culture of Fear: Why Americans Are Afraid of the Wrong Things*, 1999.

sive. The main drawback of these studies is that correlation does not prove causation: It could simply be that aggressive people prefer violent entertainment.

The weaknesses in the evidence supporting the indictment of violent entertainment are well-known to scholars in the field. For the layman, Jib Fowles, a professor of communication at the University of Houston, offers a concise, accessible overview in his 1999 book *The Case for Television Violence*.

But politicians and "public health" busybodies want to pretend that critics like Freedman and Fowles do not exist, that there is no controversy about the impact of violent entertainment. Hence the joint statement highlighted by Brownback, including the whopper about "well over 1,000 studies" and the exaggeration of what the research shows—both of which were uncritically repeated by newspapers.

"Among the professional community," said Brownback, "there's no longer any doubt about this." In other words, only the ignorant persist in questioning the causal link between violent entertainment and violent crime, which the senator compared to the link between smoking and lung cancer.

Let's be frank. For people who think government needs to do something about violence in popular culture—a diverse group that includes both "conservatives" who supposedly insist on individual responsibility and "liberals" who supposedly believe in freedom of speech—the idea that entertainment causes crime is an excuse to censor material they would find objectionable regardless of what the research indicated. . . .

After mischaracterizing the research on violent entertainment and declaring an end to the debate, the distinguished public health experts assembled by Brownback closed their statement by calling for "a more honest dialogue." OK. You first.

Explaining the Attractions of Violent Entertainment

Glenn G. Sparks and Cheri W. Sparks

Glenn G. Sparks is a professor of communication at Purdue University, and Cheri W. Sparks is a doctoral candidate in the department of psychology at Purdue University. In an excerpt from their article "Violence, Mayhem, and Horror," the two authors discuss psychological theories that have tried to explain the enduring popularity of violent entertainment. Some of these theories rely on the premise that media depictions of violence are simply enjoyable. Other theories hold that violence itself is not appealing, but that violent movies and television shows also tend to be suspenseful, feature sexually explicit scenes, or offer some other feature besides violence that makes them appealing. Finally, a third group of explanations focuses on the post-viewing effects that violent media may have on audiences. For example, horror movies may offer adolescent males an opportunity to demonstrate that they are not afraid of violent imagery.

A WOMAN HAS SEEN THE MOVIE *PULP FICTION* three times. She considers the movie to be outrageously amusing and inventively clever. Years ago, wanting others to share in this movie, she encouraged a group of graduate-school

■

friends to attend it with her. As it turned out, her friends were completely perplexed by her attraction to such a violence-packed movie. They were particularly troubled by the fact that, during the viewing, many members of the college audience screamed out their approval and clapped wildly during the most violent scenes. After the movie, the avid *Pulp Fiction* fan received a stern lecture from her friends (all budding young social psychologists) about the negative effects of exposure to this type of media stimulus. At least one of these friends had never before attended such a violent movie and he reported that he would never do so again.

When we inquire after the particular reasons why the avid fan enjoyed *Pulp Fiction*, it turns out that she reports liking it in spite of, rather than because of, several long and violent scenes (including ones featuring male rape and gory beatings). She squinted her eyes during the most violent scenes of the movie and reacts to any other movies containing graphic violence in similar eye-squinting fashion.

The *Pulp Fiction* fan is the second author of this [article]. The first author does not share her fascination with this movie, but we do share a general preference to avoid explicit depictions of bashing, beating, knifing, punching, shooting, raping, and torturing. Only in rare circumstances, in which we are quite confident in advance of the excellence of other aspects of a movie, do we risk being exposed to graphic violence.

The *Pulp Fiction* episode illustrates a number of different responses to violent entertainment. Some people may generally choose to stay away from violent movies (as was the case with the colleague who announced his intent to avoid any violent movies like *Pulp Fiction* in the future). Some may occasionally choose to view violent films and yet not find them very appealing (like most of the social psychology colleagues described above). Others appear to enjoy the violence wholeheartedly, as evidenced by the cheering crowd of university students who applauded wildly at the most violent scenes. Yet others may choose to view violent films and report enjoying them in spite of the fact that the violent scenes themselves do not bring feelings of pleasure, delight, or happy excitement (as in Cheri's case).

In this [article], we want to think about the appeal of violence by considering three distinct ways of enjoying this type of entertainment. First, one might report enjoyment for a violent movie precisely because the violent images themselves evoke pleasure. Second, one might report overall enjoyment of a violent movie but find the violent scenes themselves to be unpleasant. In this case, the enjoyment of the movie may actually be due to enjoyment of things that tend to co-occur with violence. Finally, one might report overall enjoyment for a violent movie not so much because of the inherent appeal of the images, but because of various gratifications that are indirectly related to the viewing of the images and are actually experienced after the images themselves are viewed. . . .

Violence, Mayhem, and Horror

In general, we use the term *violence* to refer specifically to images in which the actions of one or more characters brings about physical injury to another character. We use *mayhem* to refer in general to images that might potentially be associated with bodily harm, but are not clearly initiated by a particular character (explosions, natural disasters, etc.). *Horror* is reserved for the media content that seems designed to induce a state of fear or terror.

While violence, mayhem and horror (VMH) are conceptually distinct, there is also overlap between these categories. Attempts by characters to injure or harm another (violence) certainly qualify as mayhem, and horror films often contain violent images as one vehicle designed to arouse fear in viewers. But mayhem also might include such things as exploding volcanoes and subsequent lava flows, or buildings that explode even when no one is hurt as a result. Likewise, horror might involve grotesque images or anticipated outcomes that are unfavorable for the protagonist, but little explicit violence. . . .

Are Violence, Mayhem, and Horror Inherently Appealing?

One possibility is that media depictions of VMH contain properties that are inherently attractive or enjoyable. For example, some people may actually enjoy the sight of a bullet entering a body (an enjoyment manifested, perhaps, by the vocalization "Aha!"), quite apart from who shot the bullet or who suffered because of it. Or they may find the image of the White House exploding (*Independence Day*) to be aesthetically appealing in some way (the bright colors, the symmetry of the blast, etc.). One of us (Cheri) was completely captivated by the spectacle of the lava flows in the movie *Volcano*, quite apart from the way they fit into the movie's plot. The sensory appeal of the mayhem was enjoyed for its own sake and the plot details were of little concern to her. In the case of horror, individuals may specifically seek the feelings of thrill and excitement that horrific images evoke or they may be drawn in by the aesthetic appeal of scenes involving bizarre monsters. . . .

Sensory Delight. As just noted, images involving VMH may have sensory appeal. The enjoyment of the color and movement of a lava flow qualifies as an example. Some viewers may find particular sensory delight in the sound of an alien popping out of a person's stomach in the horror film *Alien*. Perhaps some are enamored with slow-motion shots of bodies being riddled with bullets and blood splashing into the air, as shown for one of the first times in movie history in the film *Bonnie and Clyde*. An important dimension of this explanation is that these sensory experiences are enjoyed completely apart from the surrounding context, characters, plot, and so on that might be happening simultaneously. . . .

Aesthetic Theory of Destruction. One account of the pleasure that may exist in viewing VMH is advanced by [V.L.] Allen and [D.B.] Greenberger. These authors explicated "an aesthetic theory of destruction" that attempts to explain the motivations involved in destructive behavior. The theory emphasizes that the same factors that contribute to aesthetic enjoyment (factors such as complexity, expectation, novelty, intensity, patterning, etc.) are also involved in destructive acts. Consequently, these authors held that there may be a powerful aesthetic pleasure elicited by acts of destruction. For example, when a pane of glass is struck by a hard object, it may or may not break. If it does break, the shattering of the glass is complex and unpredictable. The accompanying sound of the glass breaking is not exactly the same each time. These elements, the authors contended, all contribute to the enjoyment of destruction. Although the theory was formulated primarily to account for the motivations behind destructive behavior, the authors extended the basic principles to witnessing destructive acts. They stated:

> The aesthetic theory of destruction proposes that persons seek stimulation in the destruction of an object just as they seek stimulation in more socially acceptable aesthetic experiences. . . . Demolition derbies, disaster movies, and burning buildings are just a few examples of mundane situations in which persons intentionally choose to observe acts of destruction.

. . . *Novelty*. Perhaps some of the appeal of images of VMH can be explained by the fact that they are unusual or novel. The orientation to novel stimuli may have some evolutionary significance. Dangers often arise from a disruption of the status quo and those who survive best are those who can efficiently and quickly identify new and unusual events in the environment. [N.] Carroll commented on the inherent properties of horror that seem to be consistent with the idea that their appeal is found in their novelty. He stated that "horror attracts because anomalies command attention and elicit curiosity.". . .

Sensation Seeking

One explanation that incorporates components of both the sensory delight and novelty explanations is the sensation-seeking view. According to this explanation, VMH are enjoyed by some viewers because of their intrinsic capabilities to satisfy the need for arousing stimulation. One of [M.] Zuckerman's most recent [1996] statements on sensation seeking defines the concept in the following way: "Sensation seeking is a trait defined by the seeking of varied, novel, complex, and intense sensations and experiences, and the willingness to take physical, social, legal, and financial risks for the sake of such experience."

The fact that sensation seeking is related to preferences for arousing media seems to be well established. [Z.] Zaleski exposed subjects to a variety of pictures that included torture scenes, hanging, and corpses, as well as to scenes of celebration and "mild love making." High sensation seekers preferred pictures that had been rated by a different group of subjects as highly arousing—regardless of whether the content was positive or negative. They preferred a group of neutral pictures the least. In contrast, low sensation seekers preferred the negatively arousing pictures the least and positively arousing pictures the most. [D.D.] Johnston studied high school students and found sensation seeking to be related to the preference for viewing horror films. Other researchers have also reported that sensation seeking is positively correlated with the preference for media horror. As Zuckerman observed, "Sensation seekers prefer being frightened or shocked to being bored.". . .

Dispositional Alignments. One particularly satisfying explanation for the appeal of VMH is the disposition theory. According to this theory, viewers of media entertainment react to the events on the screen in much the same way that they would react to the events if they witnessed them in real life. A crucial component in such witnessing is the formation of dispositional alignments with various characters. That is, viewers form likes and dislikes for the characters involved in the drama. [Dolf] Zillmann summarized the dynamic of dispositional alignments:

> Specifically, a favorable disposition toward friendlike characters is thought to instigate hopes for benefaction and fears of aversive outcomes. Liked characters, in other words, are deemed deserving of good fortunes and undeserving of bad ones. In contrast, an unfavorable disposition toward enemylike characters is thought to instigate hopes for aversive, punitive outcomes and fears of benefaction. Disliked characters, then, are deemed deserving of bad fortunes and undeserving of good ones.

The theory of dispositional alignments has been used quite successfully to predict emotional reactions of consumers to a variety of types of entertainment. In terms of the appeal of violence, the theory suggests that the typical viewer is willing (even eager) to witness various acts of violence so long as the ones who suffer from these acts are disliked and perceived as deserving of their punishment. As Zillmann stated, "Negative affective dispositions, then, set us free to thoroughly enjoy punitive violence." . . .

Violating Social Norms

In discussing the appeal of novelty in violent entertainment, [C.] McCauley considered a view that he labeled "curiosity/fascination theory." But on close scrutiny, the curiosity or fascination of which he wrote is not so much a general curiosity or fascination but, rather, a very specific one. According to his analysis of the horror film, many of the images presented in this form of entertainment violate social norms. He states that the violation of norms "holds a fascination for people to the extent that they rarely see these violations in everyday experience.". . .

This view is not inconsistent with disposition theory. One possibility is that when viewers are encouraged through various cinematic techniques to form favorable alignments with characters who engage in rule-breaking behavior—characters who, according to mainstream social norms, might be considered to be despicable—their violent behaviors may be particularly appealing. This may be precisely the dynamic that worked in the movie *Bonnie and Clyde*. As [J.] Hoberman wrote:

> It should not be surprising then that, for some, *Bonnie and Clyde* was not so much overly violent as excessively glamorous: "Pretty people who kill, and the killing they do is pretty too," wrote Jimmy Breslin in *New York* (July 8, 1968). . . . Good looks, swell clothes, and impossible cool set Bonnie and Clyde apart from their dowdy environment. . . . These were no ordinary delinquents. . . . Bonnie and Clyde were too beautiful to grow up, become domestic, join the middle class.

So, when viewers are encouraged to form positive dispositions with characters who make a habit of violating social norms by committing aggression, then pleasure may be taken from viewing these acts.

Sex Differences Based on Evolution. In a recent review of empirical evidence, [D.M.] Buss and [T.K.] Shackelford proposed that the psychological appeal of human aggression evolved as a result of adaptation to basic problems (gaining others' resources, defending against attack, negotiating status, dealing with same-sex rivals, etc.). The authors argued that after considering these problems and the adaptive, aggressive solutions that have evolved, there is evolutionary logic for the common finding that males are more aggressive than females. If the aggressive response has evolved over thousands of years of human existence as an efficient solution to various social problems, then it follows that the stimulus features of aggression (such as those in violent entertainment) have inherent attraction as generally valued commodities. . . .

Violence Confounded with Other Variables

As the formulations specified above demonstrate, there are a number of reasons for suggesting that VMH are inherently appealing. Notwithstanding these reasons, it is also plausible to suggest that this sort of entertainment is appealing not because of the inherent properties of violent or horrific content, but because of other features that seem to be naturally confounded with their occurrence. It is very difficult to judge the overall appeal of violent or horrific movies when we do not have quality control measures—perhaps violent movies are generally of better (or worse) quality than movies that are not violent. Perhaps quality is the critical variable that drives viewing selection and enjoyment. Alternatively, perhaps violent or horrific movies have more sexual content than other films and it is the sexual content that motivates viewing and supplies enjoyment. Or, perhaps it is the suspense generally associated with violence that elicits positive feelings and motivates viewing. . . .

The Appeal of Post-Viewing Gratifications

A third general explanation for the appeal of VMH is that viewers might experience various post-viewing gratifications that are associated with these types of content. According to this formulation, viewers may not actually enjoy the watching of violent or horrific images. Instead, the appeal of this kind of entertainment is to be found in post-viewing gratifications that result in reports of overall viewing enjoyment and that motivate future encounters with the same type of material.

Catharsis. One early theory in the violence literature proposed by [S.] Feshbach advanced the notion of symbolic catharsis. According to this view, exposure to media violence had potentially therapeutic properties for individuals who were angry and who, because of this emotional state, were inclined to behave aggressively. By viewing violent entertainment, regardless of its specific association with their own emotional state, individuals would leave the entertainment experience with their pent-up aggressive tendencies purged or cleansed. In short, they would feel better and certainly less inclined to act in an aggressive fashion. Presumably, witnessing others engage in violence provided the opportunity for individuals to fantasize about their own aggressive actions. Having engaged in such fantasy, the need to actually act out their anger was significantly reduced. Of particular importance for our consideration of reasons for the appeal of violence, [R.M.] Liebert & [J.N.] Sprafkin have observed that Feshbach believed that the positive feelings resulting from fantasy aggression could become habit-forming. They stated, "If the individual is rewarded often enough for fantasy aggression (he pushes his boss off a bridge in thought and feels better afterward), he gets into the habit of using fantasy aggression to "cathart" (drain off) his aggressive feelings."

Despite its early popularity, the theory of symbolic catharsis suffered from various flaws in the studies that were presumably supportive. Most importantly, a number of other studies revealed that when angry individuals were exposed to

Violent Entertainment Is Not the Most Popular Type of Entertainment

While there seems always to have been an audience for violent enactments and portrayals, it is worth remembering that violent entertainment is not as popular as other forms of entertainment, such as comedy. Most popular entertainments are devoid of violent images. A particular violent film or video game with a violent theme may be a best-seller, but the sales of such items are greatly exceeded by the sales of nonviolent fare. Film, television, and video comedies are far more popular than those featuring violence. In [one study], *Mighty Morphin Power Rangers* was said by 26 percent of parents to be among their children's favorite TV programs, but a sitcom, *Full House*, was the favorite program of 33 percent of the children. War toys and video games with fighting themes account for a small portion of the market. Toy guns account for between 1 and 2 percent of the toy market while best-media violence, their aggressive tendencies increased, in direct opposition to the theory's major prediction. Recent [1990] studies show the same finding. Current [1993] assessments of the theory conclude that the prediction of diminished aggression after exposure to media violence was simply mistaken. . . .

Overcoming Fears

Although there is some consensus about the lack of merit of the catharsis theory in the context of purging anger by exposure to media violence, we might inquire about the merits of a catharsis-type process occurring in the context of horrific or frightening media. Could it be that one might seek out frightening entertainment as a way of attempting to overcome one's fears? If so, does such exposure provide any relief?

One of us (Cheri), found the experience of viewing *The Exorcist* unbearably scary, still reporting over 25 years later that it was the scariest movie she ever saw. In fact, she found it

---

selling video games include strategy games like Tetris and nonviolent games featuring Sonic the Hedgehog and Super Mario Brothers.

While a great many people seem attracted to—or at least not wholly repelled by—violent imagery, there may be a small audience that demands violent images in its entertainment. For some boys and men, the violence is the thing. But for many, it may be not the violence per se but other satisfactions that are its main attractants. For the majority of consumers of violent imagery, the violence is a means to ends, an acceptable device valued more for what it does than for what it is. Players who like video games with action/adventure or martial-arts themes, for example, are not necessarily attracted by the violence. These games have other features that appeal to players—their engaging fantasy, challenge, and stimulation, scorekeeping, feedback, graphics, and sound effects.

Jeffrey Goldstein, ed., *Why We Watch: The Attractions of Violent Entertainment*, 1998.

so scary that after a few weeks she went back to see it again, because she had some intuition that seeing it again would help her get over her recurring images of the possibility of people's eyes turning demon-yellow as they walked through the lounge of her undergraduate dormitory.

There is certainly some evidence that media exposure to objects that are feared can serve to reduce fear and anxiety of the same objects. The use of filmed models is a standard technique for the treatment of phobias with the supposed mechanism of the successful treatment being gradual desensitization through repeated exposure. The intuition that repeated exposure to *The Exorcist* might help to diminish the same fears induced by the first exposure to the film seems consistent with emotional desensitization, but there appears to be little empirical evidence documenting a specific desire to engage in repeat viewing for this purpose. . . .

Excitation Transfer. One explanation for the enjoyment of horror is found in Zillmann's theory of excitation transfer. According to this theory, the viewer's encounter with frightening media stimuli induces elevated levels of physiological arousal. When these encounters conclude, viewers often experience a profound sense of relief that the film is over or even a strong positive feeling in response to a plot resolution in which the horrifying threat is, at last, defeated. Since the viewer remains in an elevated state of arousal from prior fear and anxiety and since arousal intensifies whatever emotion is subjectively experienced, the feelings of relief or positive effect are subsequently intensified. The euphoric feelings that viewers sometimes report after watching frightening films are undoubtedly a function of this transfer of residual excitation from prior feelings of fright. The empirical evidence in favor of the excitation transfer effect in the context of media stimuli is solid. . . .

Mastering Threats

Zillmann and [J.B.] Weaver recently [1996] explicated another theoretical framework that helps to explain the appeal of VMH—particularly for males. According to these authors, horror films may serve as a replacement in modern culture for ancient tribal initiation rites that served to bestow the status of "protector" on males and "protectee" on females. They state,

"Adolescents of modern society have to demonstrate their compliance with societal precepts in alternative social contexts, and we suggest that going to the movies provides such a context." The authors go on to predict that watching horrific entertainment provides an opportunity for males to demonstrate their mastery over the various images. In contrast, the same entertainment provides females with an opportunity to demonstrate their relative helplessness and high levels of fear. To the extent that males and females are able to perform their appropriate roles in the context of frightening entertainment, the overall experience is pleasant. This pleasure in achieving the appropriate social displays is misconstrued as enjoyment of frightening films. Notice that this account of pleasure in the wake of media threats applies mainly to adolescents rather than other population groups. Adolescents are the ones who are most conscious of assuming their appropriate societal roles.

One conceptual advantage of this explanation for the appeal of media horror is that it fully acknowledges the experience of genuine fear reactions that the data clearly document. . . .

The emphasis on mastery of threats also explains how exposure to frightening entertainment can be enjoyed despite the fact that the content itself produces negative emotional reactions. Indeed, in order for males to experience the satisfaction that comes from mastering a threat, they must first experience the threat and its accompanying negative emotional reactions. . . .

How Popular Are Violence, Mayhem, and Horror in the Media?

Some data suggests that the popularity of violence may be over-rated, perhaps due in part to the high profile that violent entertainment has occupied on the public and political agenda. In a recent [1994] video ("The killing screens"), George Gerbner took a position that deemphasizes the popularity of violent entertainment. He said:

> Violence, in itself, is not a popular commodity. To be sure, there are some good stories and very strong stories that have a lot of violence, but their popularity does not rest in the violence. Most of the highly rated programs on television are non-violent.

We would also note that Gerbner's observation also holds for mayhem and horror. Gerbner explained the prevalence of violence in media entertainment according to its properties as a transportable marketing commodity. According to him, violence can help to liven up a boring plot scenario and can be produced relatively easily and economically. Most important, violence is easily understood by an international audience and is easily exportable. Since Gerbner contends that most media productions are made with this international audience in mind, Hollywood productions tend to contain higher levels of violence than might be expected based on domestic profits. Gerbner's observations certainly do not explain fully the prevalence and popularity of VMH, but they have some merit in putting this sort of entertainment into proper perspective. The prevalence of VMH entertainment is not necessarily a reliable gauge for its general appeal. . . .

In thinking about these three types of explanations, it is important to note that they are not generally incompatible with one another. For example, one could find evidence for the notion that violent content is appealing because of its novelty (an example of the inherent appeal of violence) while simultaneously discovering that the same content is appealing because of an engaging, dramatic, conflict-filled story (an example of the appeal arising from other variables confounded with violence). Just as one may be able to explain aggressive behavior or alcohol use by appealing simultaneously to developmental factors, biological factors, or situational factors, it may be possible to explain the appeal of VMH by including all three of the general categories that we have outlined. However, just as scholars may argue about the relative contributions of development, biology, or situation to behaviors like aggression or alcohol use, the extent to which any of our three categories may ultimately explain the appeal of violence is very much an open question and subject to the results of future research that may explore these issues.

EXAMINING POP CULTURE

Debating Screen Violence: Artistic Value vs. Societal Harm

The Cathartic Effects of Violent Films

Tevi Troy

Writer and conservative activist Tevi Troy believes that violent action movies are not as bad as critics often claim and may even benefit society. Young males enjoy these films, writes Troy, because they allow audiences to vicariously experience violence without engaging in it themselves. One of the most appealing features of most violent films is their black-and-white morality: They provide an outlet for the average viewer's anxieties about the imperfect justice of the real world. Catharsis—the relieving of emotional tensions such as anger—is achieved when the protagonist destroys the villains. The cathartic effects of action films are a major part of their appeal.

IN THE FILM *TOTAL RECALL*, ARNOLD SCHWARZE-negger puts a bullet between the eyes of the woman who has posed as his wife and deadpans, "Consider zat a divorce." Such a mixture of violence and humor is a staple of contemporary action films, as are large body counts. Some critics argue that this onslaught of casual violence is a new phenomenon invading our movie theaters.

New York Times critic Vincent Canby writes, "If you have the impression that movies today are bloodier and more brutal than ever in the past, and that body counts are skyrocketing, you are absolutely right. Inflation has hit the action-

■

Excerpted from "Faster Hollywood! Kill! Kill!" by Tevi Troy, *Reason*, July 1992. Copyright © 1992, 2001 by the Reason Foundation, 3415 S. Sepulveda Blvd., Suite 400, Los Angeles, CA 90034, www.reason.com.

adventure movie with a big slimy splat." Critics worry that all this cinematic bloodletting is creating a nation of time-bombs who will explode at the slightest provocation.

But violence in popular culture is an ancient tradition. America was a violent society before Hollywood brought that fact into our living rooms. The shootouts of the Wild West predated our mass-media culture. And while gangsters littered the streets with their rivals during the mob wars of the 1920s and 1930s, Hollywood films of that era generally did not show on-screen deaths. The mob could not have gotten its inspiration from the movies, since even gangster films such as James Cagney's *Public Enemy* had little in the way of explicit violence.

If violent movies don't produce violent people, what do they do? The answer to this question lies with the people who watch the films.

Sixteen- to twenty-five-year-old males are the target audience for most films, especially for action and horror films, the most violent genres. Imputations that all kill-movie fans are, at best, Neanderthals or, at worst, latent sociopaths completely miss the mark. Movie goers can enjoy fictional bloodshed without being tempted to engage in the real thing.

Indeed, young men may find violent films—specifically the action genre—cathartic precisely because real violence is off-limits. Jeremy Fand, a young investment analyst and kill-movie aficionado, claims that these "films represent a way of getting violence without doing it yourself. They represent a fantasy of what we would like to do but can't."

The Triumph of Good over Evil

The cathartic nature of such films stems from three sources. First, since the American legal system is often frustratingly slow, viewers enjoy the immediacy of on-screen retribution. When the villain dies, justice prevails without any plea bargains, technicalities, or bureaucratic rigmarole.

Second, the moral viewer cheers (internally or externally) the triumph of good over evil. Third, although most viewers know that the hero will eventually kill the villain, a good film builds suspense, and the hero's ultimate victory relieves that tension.

The cathartic film is often highly moral, setting forth clear-cut conceptions of right and wrong. This formula appears across many different genres: cop films (from *The French Connection* to Steven Seagal's *Out for Justice*), Schwarzenegger and Stallone muscle-fests (*Red Heat, Raw Deal, Cobra*), spy thrillers (the James Bond films), comedies (*The Hard Way*), and science fiction (*Robocop*). These movies frequently center on a lone individual who dispenses justice to the villains around him.

This cathartic formula has been especially popular since Clint Eastwood became the world's biggest film draw in the late 1960s. Although moralistic westerns with stars as diverse as John Wayne, Henry Fonda, and Gene Autry had been a theater staple for decades, Eastwood's iconoclastic loner dispensing his own brand of justice in spaghetti westerns such as *The Good, the Bad, and the Ugly* and *A Fistful of Dollars* touched a nerve. He became even more popular when, as Dirty Harry, he updated his winning combination to contemporary America's crime-ridden streets.

The public perceived that the American justice system had gone soft on criminals and that real cops could no longer adequately deal with crime. But during the course of five films

A Socially Acceptable Means of Venting Anger

Scholars Carol Stearns and Peter Stearns explain in their landmark book *Anger: The Struggle for Emotional Control in America's History* that aggressive feelings are neither more nor less common now than in the past.

What has changed, the authors relate, is that the display of hostility is decreasingly tolerated in society. People used to vent their anger unreflectingly at others held to be their inferiors. Thus husbands were permitted to aggress against spouses, parents against children, masters against servants, rich against poor, whites against blacks. With the passage of time, however, an increasingly egalitarian society has decreed—either through changing customs or changing laws—that living human beings of any sort are unfit targets for hostile impulses. . . .

spanning 18 years, Dirty Harry rid San Francisco's streets of psychos, terrorists, overzealous vigilante cops, rapists, and other riffraff.

The concern with crime also gave rise to an increased focus on weaponry. In *Lethal Weapon*, automatic-bearing Mel Gibson chides Danny Glover about his choice of pistol. Sylvester Stallone in *Cobra*, Richard Gere in *No Mercy*, and Chuck Norris in *Code of Silence* all prepare for their bloody showdowns as the camera pans their arsenals. These images counter the impression that cops are out-gunned in today's urban battlegrounds.

Action Films Have Replaced Westerns

The policeman or vigilante as hero predominated as crime films took the place of the western. Once audiences saw a tearful Native American mourning the pollution of the land, as in the famous commercial of the 1970s, they could never again cheer for John Wayne to wipe out "injuns."

Mick Martin and Marsha Potter's *Video Movie Guide 1990*

In their trenchant analysis, they explain that over the last 100 years spectator sports and media violence have evolved to provide new, safe venues for people's release of aggression.

Contemporary efforts to vent anger acceptably, they write, ". . . explain the popularity of media violence and our willingness, however reluctant, to tolerate its availability for young viewers. In various aspects of popular culture, we may implicitly recognize the need for some safe targets or symbols of violence since we seek to deny anger in so many daily interactions."

It is the need of people to release their aggressions in newly-redefined permissible ways that has made television fantasy violence popular. Media sources, in their pursuit of large audiences, have obligingly provided the sought-after content.

Jib Fowles, *Television Quarterly*, Spring 1996.

reveals only 31 westerns released in the 1980s. The average cinema goer would probably recognize only five: *Heaven's Gate, Long Riders, Pale Rider, Silverado,* and *Young Guns.* Of these, *Heaven's Gate* was note-worthy only because it died at the box office and bankrupted United Artists. None of the five have any conflicts with Indians. The trend is toward the "politically correct" villain, usually a greedy white landowner or developer.

With the demise of the western, the action genre came to rest mostly in the hands of 20th-century crime fighters. Joel Silver is probably the most successful producer of this type of film. His movies follow an unerring formula: The line between right and wrong is clearly drawn, the good guy must buck the system to do his job, and, in the end, the good guy gets the villain.

Morality Plays

Like Eastwood, Silver's characters disdain bureaucracy and technicalities that free criminals. In Silver-produced films such as *Die Hard,* the *Lethal Weapon* series, and *The Last Boy Scout,* underdog individuals or motley misfits triumph over evil. His films are violent, but the death of innocents makes the audience wince, while the deaths of villains elicit cheers. When shot, good guys feel pain, bad guys disappear. In a world of grays, these black-and-white morality plays have tremendous appeal.

Contrary to its critics' assertions, movie violence has a long history and potentially beneficial effects. And, like it or not, violence is entertaining; Americans enjoy it. In this respect, violence is even simpler than its enemies claim, and a damned good show, too.

In Praise of Fictional Violence

Andrew Klavan

Andrew Klavan is the author of several novels, including the horror thriller *The Uncanny* and the suspense novel *True Crime*. In this excerpt from an article he wrote for the *Boston Review*, Klavan defends depictions of violence in popular entertainment. Klavan notes that violent stories strike deep emotional chords with audiences, and argues that this is because such stories tap into people's repressed or subconscious fascination with bloodshed. However, Klavan does not feel that people's enjoyment of violent entertainment is necessarily harmful. Instead, he believes that critics who try to connect media violence with real-life violence are more dangerous, because they blur the line between fiction and reality and turn society's attention away from more plausible causes of violent crime such as poverty and intrafamily abuse.

I LOVE THE SOUND OF PEOPLE SCREAMING. Women screaming—with their clothes torn—as they run down endless hallways with some bogeyman in hot pursuit. Men, in their priapic cars, screaming as the road ends, as the fender plummets towards fiery oblivion under their wild eyes. Children? I'm a little squeamish about children, but okay, sure, I'll take screaming children too. And I get off on gunshots—machine gun shots goading a corpse into a posthumous jitterbug; and the coital jerk and plunge of a butcher knife; and axes; even claws, if you happen to have them.

■

Excerpted from "The Shrieking of the Lambs," by Andrew Klavan, *Boston Review*, Summer 1994. Reprinted with permission from the author.

Only in Stories

Yes, yes, yes, only in stories. Of course; in fictions only: novels, TV shows, films. I've loved the scary, gooey stuff since I was a child. I've loved monsters, shootouts, bluddy murther; Women In Jeopardy (as they say in Hollywood); the slasher in the closet; the intruder's shadow that spreads up the bedroom wall like a stain. And now, having grown to man's estate, I make a very good living writing these things: thriller novels like *Don't Say A Word*, which begins with a nice old lady getting dusted and ends with an assault on a child, and *The Animal Hour* which features a woman's head being severed and stuffed into a commode.

Is it vicious? Disgusting? Sexist? Sick? Tough luck, it's my imagination—sometimes it is—and it's my readers' too—always, for all I know. And when they and I get together, when we dodge down that electric alleyway of the human skull where only murder is delight—well then, my friend, it's showtime.

But enough about me, let's talk about death. Cruel death, sexy death, exciting death: death, that is, on the page and on the screen. Because this is not a defense of violence in fiction, it's a celebration of it. And not a moment too soon either.

Hard as it is for a sane man to believe, fictional violence is under attack. Again. . . . This year's [1994's] list of would-be censors trying to shoulder their way to the trough of celebrity is hardly worth enumerating: their 15 minutes might be up by the time I'm done. Film critic Michael Medved says cinematic violence is part of a pop culture "war on traditional values"; Congressman Edward Markey says television violence should be reduced or regulated; some of our less thoughtful feminists tried to quash the novel *American Psycho* because of its descriptions of violence toward women and even some more thoughtful, like Catherine MacKinnon, have fought for censorship in law, claiming that written descriptions of "penises slamming into vaginas" deprive actual human beings of their civil rights.

It's nonsense mostly, but it has the appeal of glamour, of flash. The "issue" of fictional violence lifts crime out of the impoverished, muddy-minded, rage-filled milieus in which it usually occurs, and superimposes it on the gaudy images manufactured in Hollywood and Manhattan. Instead of trying to understand the sad, banal, ignorant souls who generally pull the trigger in our society, we get to discuss Hannibal Lecter, Ice-T, penises, vaginas. It makes for good sound bytes, anyway—the all-American diet of 15 second thoughts.

But Britain—where I've come to live because I loathe real guns and political correctness—is far from exempt. Indeed, perhaps nowhere has there been a more telling or emblematic attack on fictional violence than is going on here right now. It is a textbook example of how easily pundits and politicians can channel honest grief and rage at a true crime into a senseless assault on the innocent tellers of tales.

The Murder of Jamie Bulger

It began here this time with the killing of a child by two other children. On 12 February [1994], Jamie Bulger, a two-year-old toddler, was led out of a Merseyside shopping mall by two ten-year-olds—two little boys. The boys prodded and carried and tugged the increasingly distraught baby past dozens of witnesses who did not understand what they were seeing. When they reached a deserted railroad embankment, the two boys tortured, mutilated, and finally killed their captive for no reasons that anyone has been able to explain. . . .

The nation's search for an answer, its grief and disgust, its sense of social despair, did not resolve themselves upon a single issue until the trial judge pronounced sentence. "It is not for me to pass judgment on their upbringing," Mr. Justice Morland said of the boys as he sentenced them to be detained at Her Majesty's pleasure. "But I suspect exposure to violent video films may in part be an explanation."

No one knew why he said such a thing. There had been speculation in some of the papers that *Child's Play 3*, which had been rented by one of the killers' fathers, had given the son ideas. But there was no testimony at the trial, no evidence presented showing that the boy had seen it or that it had had a contributing effect. . . .

It didn't matter. As far as journalists were concerned, as far as public debate was concerned, "video nasties," as they are called here, became the central issue of the case. Forget the subconscious, the broken home, the poverty, the family cruelty, the breakdown of western society, even the trials of masculinity and the moral energy stuff. For the next few days, the newspapers were splattered with stories about *Child's Play 3*. . . .

A Complex Relationship

Now, I would not say that my fictions—any fictions—have no effect on real life. Or that books, movies and TV are mere regurgitations of what's going on in the society around them. . . . Rather, the relationship between fiction and humanity's unconscious is so complex, so resonant, and even stichomythic that it is impossible to isolate one from the other in terms of cause and effect. . . .

Fiction and reality do interact, but we don't know how, not at all. And since we don't understand the effect of one upon the other . . . whence arises this magical certainty that violence in fiction begets violence in real life like one of those old 3D films that promised to "leap off the screen"?

The answer seems to come straight out of the pages of Sigmund Freud. Or St. Paul if you prefer: "Wherein thou judgest another, thou condemnest thyself." It's Psychology 1A, but that doesn't negate the truth of it: that pleasure which is unknowingly repressed is outwardly condemned. The censor always attacks the images that secretly appeal to him or her the most. The assault on violent fiction is not really an attempt to root out the causes of violence—no one can seriously believe that. The attempt to censor fictional violence is a guilt-ridden slap at ourselves, in the guise of a mythical *them*, for taking such pleasure in make-believe acts that, in real life, would be reprehensible. How—we seem to be asking ourselves—how, in a world in which Jamie Bulger dies so young, can we kick back with a beer at night and enjoy a couple of hours of *Child's Play 3*? . . .

How can we enjoy this stuff so much? So very much. Not all of us perhaps. I'm forever being told that there are people who'd rather not take violence with their fiction—although I wonder how many would say so if you included the delicate violence of an Agatha Christie or the "literary" violence of, say, Hemingway and Faulkner. But even if we accept the exceptions, even if we limit the field to real gore, it does seem to me that the numbers are incredible, the attraction truly profound. . . .

Once, I picked out what looked like a cheap horror novel by

an author I'd never heard of. . . . I asked every reader I knew if they had ever heard of the book, *Salem's Lot,* or its author, Stephen King. None of them had. . . . Later, the movie *Carrie* helped launch what has to be one of the most successful novelistic careers since Dickens. But even before that, all over the country, all over the world eventually, readers . . . were steadily discovering the nausea and mayhem and terror of the man's vision.

People Simply Enjoy Fictional Violence

The moral, I mean, is this: To construct a bloodsoaked nightmare of unrelenting horror is not an easy thing. But if you build it, they will come. And so the maker of violent fiction—ho, ho—he walks among us in Nietzschean glee. He has bottled the Dionysian whirlwind and is selling it as a soft drink. . . . Like deep-browed Homer, when he told of a spear protruding from a man's head with an eyeball fixed to the point, the violent storyteller knows that that gape of disgust on your respectable mug is really the look of love. You may denounce him, you may even censor him. . . . But sooner or later, in one form or another, he knows you'll show up to see and listen to him. . . .

Fiction lives or dies, not on its messages, but on the depth and power of the emotional experience it provides. . . . An enormous amount of intellectual energy seems to have been expended in a failed attempt to suppress the central, disturbing and irreducible fact of this experience: it's fun. Like sex: it's lots of fun. We watch fictional people love and die and screw and suffer and weep for our pleasure. It gives us joy.

And we watch them kill too. And this seems to give us as much joy as anything. All right, I suppose you can talk about the catharsis of terror, or the harmless release of our violent impulses. Those are plausible excuses, I guess. It doesn't take a genius to notice how often—practically always—it's the villain of a successful piece of violent art who becomes its icon. Hannibal Lecter and Leatherface, Freddy Kreuger and Dracula—these are the posters that go up on the wall, the characters that we remember. . . .

So I suppose, if you must, you could say these creatures represent our buried feelings. Whether it's Medea or Jason (from *Friday the 13th*), the character who commits acts of savage violence always has the appeal of a Caliban: that thing of darkness that must be acknowledged as our own. Not that people are essentially violent, but that they are violent among other things and the violence has to be repressed. . . . Some emotions must be repressed and repressed emotions return via the imagination in distorted and inflated forms: that's the law of benevolent hypocrisy, the law of civilized life. It is an unstated underpinning of utopian thought . . . that the repressed can be eliminated completely or denied or happily freed or remolded with the proper education. It can't. Forget about it. Cross it off your list of things to do. The monsters are always there in their cages. As Stephen King says, with engaging simplicity, his job is to take them out for a walk every now and then.

But again, this business of violent fiction as therapy—this modern-jargon version of Aristotle—it's a defense, isn't it, as if these stories needed a reason for being. In order to celebrate violent fiction—I mean, *celebrate* it—it's the joy you've got to talk about. The joy of cruelty, the thrill of terror, the adrenaline of the hunter, the heartbeat of the deer—all reproduced in the safe playground of art. A joy indeed. . . .

Delight vs. Guilt

When it comes to our messier, our somehow unseemly, pleasures, like fictional gore, we are downright embarrassed by our delight. But delight is certainly what it is. Nubile teens caught out *in flagrante* by a nutcase in a hockey mask? You bet it's erotic. Whole families tortured to death by a madman who's traced them through their vacation photos. Ee-yewwww. Goblins who jump out of the toilet to devour you ass first. Delightful stuff. . . .

And we've always been that way. The myths of our ancient gods, the lives of our medieval saints, the entertainments of our most civilized cultures have always included healthy doses of rape, cannibalism, evisceration, and general mayhem. Critics like Michael Medved complain that never before has it all been quite so graphic, especially on screen. We are becoming "desensitized" to bloodshed, he claims, and require more and more gore to excite our feelings. But when have human beings ever been particularly "sensitized" to fictional violence? The technology to create the illusion of bloodshed has certainly improved, but read *Titus Andronicus* with its wonderful stage direction, "Enter a messenger with two heads and a hand," read the orgasmic staking of Lucy in *Dracula*, read de Sade, for crying out loud. There were always some pretty good indications of which way we'd go once we got our hands on the machinery.

Because we love it. It makes us do a little inner dance of excitement, tension, and release. . . . Violent fiction with its graver purposes, if any, concealed—fiction unadorned with overt messages or historical significance—rubs our noses in the fact that narratives of horror, murder, and gore are a blast, a gas. When Freddy Kreuger disembowels someone in a geyser of blood, when Hannibal Lecter washes down his victim with a nice Chianti—the only possible reason for this nonreal, non-meaningful event to occur is that it's going to afford us pleasure. Which leaves that pleasure obvious, exposed. It's the exposure, not the thrill, the censors want to get rid of. Again: celebration is the only defense.

Disturbing Trends

And yet—I know—while I celebrate, the new, not-very-much-improved Rome is burning. Last year sometime, I had a conversation with a highly intelligent Scottish filmmaker who had just returned from New York. Both of us had recently seen Sylvester Stallone's mountaineering action picture *Cliffhanger*. I'd seen it in the placid upper class neighborhood of South Kensington, he'd seen it in a theater in Times Square. I had been thrilled by the movie's special effects and found the hilariously dopey script sweetly reminiscent of the comic books I'd read as a child. My friend had found the picture grimly disturbing. The Times Square theater had been filled with rowdy youths. Every time the bad guys killed someone, the youths cheered—and when a woman was murdered, they howled with delight.

I freely confess that I would have been unable to enjoy the movie under those circumstances. Too damned noisy for one thing. And, all right, yes, as a repression fan, I could only get off on the cruelty of the villains insofar as it fired my anticipation of the moment when Sly would cut those suckers down. Another audience could just as easily have been cheering the murders of Jews in *Schindler's List* or of blacks in *Mississippi Burning*. I understand that, and it would be upsetting and frightening to be surrounded by a crowd which seemed to have abandoned the non-negotiable values.

Michael Medved believes—not that one film produces one vicious act—but that a ceaseless barrage of anti-religion, anti-family, slap-happy-gore films and fictions has contributed to the erosion of values so evident on 42nd Street. I don't know whether this is true or not—neither does he—but, as with the judge's remarks in the Bulger case, it strikes me as a very suspicious place to start. . . . Surely, the Scotsman's story illustrates that the problem lies not on the screen but in the seats, in the lives that have produced that audience. Fiction cannot make of people what life has not, good or evil. . . .

But more to the point: though the Times Square crowd's reaction was scary—rude too—it was not necessarily harmful in itself, either to them or me. For all I know, it was a beneficial release of energy and hostility, good for the mental health. And in any case, it took place in the context of their experience of a fiction and so (outside of the unmannerly noise they made) was beyond my right to judge, approve, or condemn. Nobody has to explain his private pleasures to me.

Fiction and Reality Are Different

Because fiction and reality are different. It seems appalling that anyone should have to say it, but it does need to be said. Fiction is not subject to the same moral restrictions as real life. It should remain absolutely free because, at whatever level, it is, like sex, a deeply personal experience engaged in by consent in the hope of anything from momentary release to satori. Like sex, it is available to fools and creeps and monsters, and that's life; that's tough. Because fiction is, like sex, at the core of our individual humanity. Stories are the basic building blocks of spiritual maturity. No one has any business messing with them. No one at all.

Reality, on the other hand, needs its limits, maintained by force if necessary, for the simple reason that there are actions that directly harm the safety and liberty of other people. They don't merely offend them; they don't just threaten their delicate sense of themselves; they *hurt* them—really, painfully, a lot. Again, it seems wildly improbable that this should be forgotten, but Americans' current cultural discussions show every evidence that it has been. Just as fictions are being discussed as if they were actions . . . , actual crimes and atrocities are being discussed as if they were cultural events, subject to aesthetic considerations. Trial lawyers won a lesser conviction for lady-killer Robert Chambers by claiming his victim was promiscuous; columnists defended dick-chopper Lorena Bobbit, saying it might be all right to mutilate a man in his sleep, provided he was a really nasty guy. The fellows who savaged Reginald Denny during the LA riots claim they were just part of the psychology of the mob. And the Menendez brothers based much of their defense on a portrayal of themselves as victims, a portrayal of their victims as abusers. These are all arguments appropriate to fiction only. Only in fiction are crimes mitigated by symbolism and individuals judged not for what they've done but because of what they represent. . . .

Fiction and real life must be distinguished from one another. The radical presumption of fiction is play, the radical presumption of real life is what Martin Amis called "the gentleness of human flesh." If we have lost the will to defend that gentleness, then God help us, because consigning Chucky to the flames is not going to bring it back.

The Sanctity of Human Life

One of the very best works of violent fiction to come along in the last few years is Thomas Harris's novel, *The Silence of the Lambs.* The story, inspired, like *Psycho*, by the real-life case of murderer Ed Gein, concerns the hunt for the serial killer Jame Gumb, a failed transsexual, who strips his female victims' flesh in order to create a woman costume in which he can clothe himself. . . .

When Harris introduces the killer's next victim—Catherine Martin—he presents us with a character whom we aren't meant to like very much. Rich, spoiled, arrogant, dissolute, Catherine is admirable only for the desperate cleverness she shows in her battle to stay alive. But for the rest of the novel—the attempt to rescue Catherine before it's too late—Harris depends on our fear for her, our identification with her, our deep desire to see her get out of this in one piece. . . .

He relies on our irrational—spiritual—conviction that Catherine, irritating though she may be, must not be killed because . . . for no good reason: because she Must Not. Harris knowingly taps in to the purely emotional imperative we share with the book's heroine, Clarice Starling [the FBI agent who's trying to crack the case]: like her, we won't be able to sleep until the screaming of innocent lambs is stopped. Harris makes pretty well sure of it.

At the end, in the only injection of auctorial opinion in the book, Harris wryly notes that the scholarly journals which include articles on the Gumb case never use the words *crazy* or *evil* in their discussions of the killer. The intellectual world is uncomfortable with the inherent Must-Not, the instinctive absolute, and the individual responsibility those words ultimately suggest. . . . Harris, I think, is trying to argue that if we don't trust our mindless belief in the sanctity of human life, we produce monsters that the sleep of reason never dreamed of. *The Silence of the Lambs*, as the title suggests, is a dramatization of a world in which the spirit has lost its power to speak.

We live in that world, no question. . . . With our culture atomizing, we think we can make up enough rules, impose enough restrictions, inject enough emptiness into our language to replace the shared moral conviction that's plainly gone. I think all stories—along with being fun—have the potential to humanize precisely because the richest fun of them is dependent on our identification with their characters. . . . But stories can't do for us what experience hasn't. They're just not that powerful. . . . And if some people are living lives in our society that make them unfit for even the most shallow thrills of fiction, you can't solve that problem by eliminating the fiction; it doesn't even begin to make sense. By allowing politicians and pundits to turn our attention to "the problem of fictional violence," we are really allowing them to make us turn our backs on the problems of reality. . . .

After a crime like the Jamie Bulger murder, we should be asking ourselves a million questions: about our abandonment of family life, about our approach to poverty and unemployment, about the failures of our educational systems—about who and what we are and the ways we treat each other, the things we do and omit to do. These are hard, sometimes boring questions. But when instead we let our discussions devolve, as they have, into this glamour-rotten debate on whether people should be able to enjoy whatever fiction they please, then we make meaningless the taking of an individual's life. And that's no fun at all.

Common Defenses of Media Violence—and Their Flaws

Rosalind Silver

Rosalind Silver is a freelance writer and the former editor of *Media & Values* magazine, in which this article originally appeared. In it she discusses the enduring problem of media violence. To deal with the issue, she writes, the public must reject the simplistic arguments that are commonly used to defend violent entertainment. She contends that media violence is more graphic than it has been in the past; that society should aid parents in limiting their children's exposure to media violence; that the TV industry intentionally uses violent programs to attract viewers; and that movie and television producers have a responsibility to reduce the amount of violence in popular entertainment. These are necessary steps, Silver concludes, toward creating a less violent culture.

"The three networks predicted a lessening of violence in programming. Ten years later it's hundred times worse."
—Sen. Thomas J. Dodd, 1964

WITH ALMOST CLOCKWORK REGULARITY, EVERY 10 years since the introduction of television, Congress has held hearings on the impact of media violence. Repeatedly, media

■

Reprinted from "Challenging the Myths of Media Violence," by Rosalind Silver, *Media & Values*, 1994, by permission of the Center for Media Literacy, Los Angeles.

researchers have testified to the mounting evidence linking media portrayals of violence to aggressive behavior. At every hearing, entertainment industry executives completed the ritual by complaining that the connections could not be proved.

Past Reforms Have Failed

Coming as they did in a long hot summer of concern about escalating societal violence, the 1993 series of hearings caused more than an average amount of industry soul searching and defensiveness. The actions that may yet result remain unclear, although suggested ideas include ratings reform, more sophisticated media monitoring systems, V-chips and other technological devices and the threat of regulation.

In the past, remedies have either not been implemented or have not lasted. Cutting back on media violence has been like swearing off junk food. Sooner or later, the commercial attractions of blood and gore were too tempting, and violent programming once again became a major part of the media menu.

Perhaps the problem lies in trying to isolate a single "solution." The delusion that there is some magic quick fix that can undo decades of decline in social mores and civic virtue—as well as broadcasting regulation and responsibility—is typical, however, of the instant-gratification culture that television has spawned.

There is no one solution to violence.

The parameters of the problem of media violence are many and complex. The resolution must also be multi-layered and cumulative. Indeed, there is not one solution but only the search for solutions which, like any effort at systematic change can be begun today, but will never be finished.

The Media Literacy Movement

Yes, V-chips may be useful in some families. And the rating system could use some improvements. Self-discipline on the part of the industry is the decent thing for corporate citizens of today's media culture to do, but even that won't cure the systemic nature of violence that now haunts our national psyche.

A new resource we've not had in previous decades is the burgeoning media literacy movement. Media literacy provides the framework not just for analyzing what we see but also for understanding the role media has in our culture and taking personal and public action to challenge that role when it intrudes on the common good. Applying media literacy principles and methods to the problem of media violence opens up new possibilities for each of us to first define the situation in our own lives and secondly to learn and apply ways to change it if we wish.

Perhaps more importantly, media literacy can give us the tools to challenge the five myths of media violence, those key arguments that prop up the defense for violence in media. We hear them among respected friends, thoughtful parents, entertainment industry professionals, op-ed writers. Some of them sound logical on their face. But like other myths, they actually represent tired attempts to avoid critical thinking. They support a dangerous status quo and provide excuses for a crucial lack of responsibility for the public health crisis we are facing as a culture. It's time to end forever these worn-out myths.

Television Is More Violent Now than in the Past

1. I watched TV violence when I was a child and I turned out OK. It's true that not every babyboomer who watched early cartoons, *The Untouchables* or Frankenstein films grew up to be a serial killer. But media violence is different now and so is the culture in which our children view it. Not only are depictions of violence far more graphic and gory today thanks to special effects and computer animation techniques but violence in current media serves to validate a culture that is already violent as a result of poverty, drugs, unemployment and the ready availability of guns. Furthermore the in-your-face attitudes of pranksters like Beavis and Butt-head present not just violent behavior but cynical attitudes about the meaning of life, the value of community and the dignity of the human person.

Of far more consequence, perhaps, than worrying about whether children will become serial killers are the three other effects of media violence that recent researchers have identified: feeling fearful (the victim effect); turning their backs on those in need (bystander effect); and having an increasing appetite for violence all their lives.

2. Violence in the media just reflects violence in society.

Yes, art reflects life. Producers of newsmagazines and reality shows, movies of the week and theatrical films carefully monitor the news for real-life stories that might make dramatic programming. Unfortunately, they are convinced—with justification—that violence succeeds better than other programming in capturing viewers' attention.

But in fact TV and films depict much more violence than exists in real life. No one experiences the kind of routine violence (five acts of violence per hour in prime time; 25 or more in children's shows) that is depicted on TV every day. This sensational violence has a leading effect on society. Ever more violent programming and films contribute to escalating amounts of violence in society. The real-life violence is then reprocessed by media producers into new, more violent programs. It's time to stop this cycle of violence.

Society Must Help Parents

3. Decisions about viewing violence should be up to the parents. In this century, the mass media have come to rival parents, school and religion as the most influential institution in children's lives. In fact, one study indicates that teenagers are more likely to believe the media than their parents when the two disagree. Most parents try to insure that outside influences—teachers, friends, relatives—are positive influences on their children. But the stream of media that flows into the average household is overwhelming.

Those who are parents today have a daunting task. Unlike parents of the past, they must acquire new media management techniques to protect their children from harm along with media literacy skills that will teach the next generation self-discipline, critical evaluation and self-awareness. But parents today also have a right to expect society to support their child-rearing efforts with a healthy physical, intellectual, spiritual and cultural environment.

4. Violence is a natural part of drama. Somehow Shakespeare always comes up at this point. Yes, he was a great playwright, but the best of his plays retain their impact because their violent climates are accompanied by skillful character development and what media scholar Brian Stonehill calls "a sense of the preciousness and fragility of life." Conversely,

Stonehill notes, much of today's mass media crime fare "makes us feel that life is cheap and disposable."

What drama does require is not so much violence as conflict, which is best when viewers can relate it to the circumstances of their own lives. Violence is not the only way to solve conflict in even the best of dramas.

The First Amendment Does Not Protect All Speech

5. Media producers should be free to create any images they want. After all, that's what the U.S. Constitution provides. The political and artistic freedom guaranteed by the First Amendment is indeed a resource to treasure. But it was never intended to completely eliminate all forms of social control over expression. Long ago jurists decided that free speech did not protect the right "to shout fire in a crowded theater."

Movie and television producers must be able to create what they envision. But because we live in a systematically violent culture, it seems irresponsible for the creative community to allow their imaginations unbridled rein, put the images out there and walk away, saying: "I'm an artist so I have no responsibility for how my images affect society."

We do need to be cautious in how we interpret this principle in regard to popular media. But while we wait for judicial wheels to grind slowly, media literacy education in schools and churches and community centers can shape public opinion to influence the media marketplace without the need for Congressional or other government regulation.

Building a Less Violent Culture

With these myths exploded we can begin the task of building a new, less violent culture.

With our society in crisis, it's no time to sit on the sidelines. We must break the cycle of blame and accusation on this issue. If there is to be a future for any of us, we must create a culture where our children can grow up safe, healthy and whole. But we can't do it waiting for someone else. If we want there to be "peace on earth,"—as well as an end to media violence—we must also remember the second line of the song: "so let it begin with me."

Marketing Violence to Children

Federal Trade Commission

In June 1999, in response to the April 20, 1999, school shootings in Littleton, Colorado, in which two teenagers killed thirteen people at Columbine High School, President Bill Clinton commissioned a study on whether the entertainment industry markets violent content to minors. In September 2000 the Federal Trade Commission (FTC), the government agency charged with promoting free-market competition and monitoring unfair trade practices, released its report on the marketing of violent media to children and teenagers. In the executive summary of the report, excerpted below, the FTC states that the entertainment industry intentionally targets advertising for violent movies, television shows, and video games at children under seventeen. The FTC proposes that regulatory codes be expanded to prohibit the advertising of violent media and recommends that the ratings systems for violent entertainment be better enforced.

ON JUNE 1, 1999, PRESIDENT CLINTON ASKED THE Federal Trade Commission and the Department of Justice to undertake a study of whether the movie, music recording, and computer and video game industries market and advertise products with violent content to youngsters. The President's request paralleled Congressional calls for such a study. The President raised two specific questions: Do the industries promote products they themselves acknowledge warrant parental

■

From the Executive Summary of the Federal Trade Commission's report *Marketing Violent Entertainment to Children*, September 2000, found at www.ftc.gov/opa/2000/09/youthviol.htm.

caution in venues where children make up a substantial percentage of the audience? And are these advertisements intended to attract children and teenagers?

For all three segments of the entertainment industry, the answers are plainly "yes."

Although the motion picture, music recording and electronic game industries have taken steps to identify content that may not be appropriate for children, companies in those industries routinely target children under 17 as the audience for movies, music and games that their own rating or labeling systems say are inappropriate for children or warrant parental caution due to their violent content. Moreover, children under 17 frequently are able to buy tickets to R-rated movies without being accompanied by an adult and can easily purchase music recordings and electronic games that have a parental advisory label or are restricted to an older audience. The practice of pervasive and aggressive marketing of violent movies, music and electronic games to children undermines the credibility of the industries' ratings and labels. Such marketing also frustrates parents' attempts to make informed decisions about their children's exposure to violent content.

Media Violence Does Influence Children

For years—over backyard fences and water coolers, on talk radio and in academic journals—parents, social scientists, criminologists, educators, policymakers, health care providers, journalists and others have struggled to understand how and why some children turn to violence. The dialogues took on new urgency with the horrifying school shooting on April 20, 1999, in Littleton, Colorado.

Scholars and observers generally have agreed that exposure to violence in entertainment media alone does not cause a child to commit a violent act and that it is not the sole, or even necessarily the most important, factor contributing to youth aggression, anti-social attitudes and violence. Nonetheless, there is widespread agreement that it is a cause for concern. The Commission's literature review reveals that a majority of the investigations into the impact of media violence on children find that there is a high correlation between exposure to media violence and aggressive, and at times violent, behavior. In addition, a number of research efforts report that exposure to media violence is correlated with increased acceptance of violent behavior in others, as well as an exaggerated perception of the amount of violence in society.

Industry Self-Regulation

For their part, the entertainment industries have recognized these concerns and taken steps to alert parents to violent or explicit content through self-regulatory product rating or labeling programs. Self-regulation by these industries is especially important considering the First Amendment protections that prohibit government regulation of content in most instances.

The self-regulatory programs of the motion picture, music recording and electronic game industries each address violence, as well as sexual content, language, drug use and other explicit content that may be of concern to parents. In keeping with the President's request, the Commission focused on the marketing of entertainment products designated as violent under these systems. In its analysis, the Commission accepted each industry's determination of whether a particular motion picture, music recording or electronic game contains violent content; the Commission did not examine the content itself.

The motion picture industry uses a rating board to rate virtually all movies released in the United States, requires the age-related rating to appear in advertising and makes some effort to review ads for rated movies to ensure that their content is suitable for general audiences. The music recording industry recommends the use of a general parental advisory label on music with "explicit content." The decision to place a parental advisory label on a recording is made by the artist and the music publishing company and involves no independent third-party review; nor does the industry provide for any review of marketing and advertising. In late August 2000, the recording industry trade association recommended that recording companies not advertise explicit-content labeled recordings in media outlets with a majority under-17 audience. The electronic game industry requires games to be labeled with age- and content-based rating information and requires that the rating information appear in advertising. Only the electronic game industry has adopted a rule prohibiting its marketers from targeting advertising for games to children below the age designations indicated by the rating.

Products Rated for Adults Are Marketed to Children

The Commission carefully examined the structure of these rating and labeling systems, and studied how these self-regulatory systems work in practice. The Commission found that despite the variations in the three industries' systems, the outcome is consistent: individual companies in each industry routinely market to children the very products that have the industries' own parental warnings or ratings with age restrictions due to their violent content. Indeed, for many of these products, the Commission found evidence of marketing and media plans that expressly target children under 17. In addition, the companies' marketing and media plans showed strategies to promote and advertise their products in the media outlets most likely to reach children under 17, including those television programs ranked as the "most popular" with the under-17 age group, such as *Xena: Warrior Princess*, *South Park* and *Buffy the Vampire Slayer*; magazines and Internet sites with a majority or substantial (*i.e.*, over 35 percent) under-17 audience, such as *Game Pro*, *Seventeen* and *Right On!*, as well as *mtv.com*, *ubl.com* and *happypuppy.com*; and teen hangouts, such as game rooms, pizza parlors and sporting apparel stores.

Movies. Of the 44 movies rated R for violence the Commission selected for its study, the Commission found that 35, or 80 percent, were targeted to children under 17. Marketing plans for 28 of those 44, or 64 percent, contained express statements that the film's target audience included children under 17. For example, one plan for a violent R-rated film stated, "Our goal was to find the elusive teen target audience and make sure everyone between the ages of 12-18 was exposed to the film." Though the marketing plans for the remaining seven R-rated films did not expressly identify an under-17 target audience, they led the Commission to conclude that children under 17 were targeted nonetheless. That is, the plans were either extremely similar to the plans of the films that did identify an under-17 target audience, or they detailed actions synonymous with targeting that age group, such as promoting the film in high schools or in publications with majority under-17 audiences.

Music. Of the 55 music recordings with explicit content labels the Commission selected for its study, marketing plans for 15, or 27 percent, expressly identified teenagers as part of their target audience. One such plan, for instance, stated that its "Target audience" was "Alternative/urban, rock, pop, hardcore—12–34." The marketing documents for the remaining 40 explicit-content labeled recordings examined did not expressly state the age of the target audience, but they detailed the same methods of marketing as the plans that specifically identified teens as part of their target audience, including placing advertising in media that would reach a majority or substantial percentage of children under 17.

Games. Of the 118 electronic games with a Mature rating for violence the Commission selected for its study, 83, or 70 percent, targeted children under 17. The marketing plans for 60 of these, or 51 percent, expressly included children under 17 in their target audience. For example, one plan for a game rated Mature for its violent content described its "target audience" as "Males 12–17—Primary Males 18–34—Secondary." Another plan referred to the target market as "Males 17–34 due to M rating (the true target is males 12–34)." Documents for the remaining 23 games showed plans to advertise in magazines or on television shows with a majority or substantial under-17 audience. Most of the plans that targeted an under-17 audience set age 12 as the younger end of the spectrum, but a few plans for violent Mature-rated games targeted children as young as six.

Ratings Systems Have Been Ineffective

Further, most retailers make little effort to restrict children's access to products with violent content. Surveys conducted for the Commission in May through July 2000 found that just over half the movie theaters admitted children ages 13 to 16 to R-rated films even when not accompanied by an adult. The Commission's surveys also indicate that unaccompanied children have various strategies to see R-rated movies when theaters refuse to sell them tickets. Additionally, the Commission's surveys showed that unaccompanied children ages 13 to

16 were able to buy both explicit content recordings and Mature-rated electronic games 85 percent of the time.

Although consumer surveys show that parents value the existing rating and labeling systems, they also show that parents' use and understanding of the systems vary. The surveys also consistently reveal high levels of parental concern about violence in the movies, music and video games their children see, listen to and play. These concerns can only be heightened by the extraordinary degree to which young people today are immersed in entertainment media, as well as by recent technological advances such as realistic and interactive video games. The survey responses indicate that parents want and welcome help in identifying which entertainment products might not be suitable for their children.

Better Enforcement of Ratings Systems Is Needed

Since the President requested this study over a year ago, each of the industries reviewed has taken positive steps to address these concerns. Nevertheless, the Commission believes that all three industries should take additional action to enhance their self-regulatory efforts. The industries should:

1. *Establish or expand codes that prohibit target marketing to children and impose sanctions for violations.* All three industries should improve the usefulness of their ratings and labels by establishing codes that prohibit marketing R-rated/M-rated/explicit-labeled products in media or venues with a substantial under-17 audience. In addition, the Commission suggests that each industry's trade associations monitor and encourage their members' compliance with these policies and impose meaningful sanctions for non-compliance.

2. *Increase compliance at the retail level.* Restricting children's retail access to entertainment containing violent content is an essential complement to restricting the placement of advertising. This can be done by checking identification or requiring parental permission before selling tickets to R movies, and by not selling or renting products labeled "Explicit" or rated R or M, to children.

3. *Increase parental understanding of the ratings and labels.* For parents to make informed choices about their children's

entertainment, they must understand the ratings and the labels, as well as the reasons for them. That means the industries should all include the reasons for the rating or the label in advertising and product packaging and continue their efforts to educate parents—and children—about the meanings of the ratings and descriptors. Industry should also take steps to better educate parents about the ratings and labels.

Industry Self-Regulation Is Not Censorship

The Commission emphasizes that its review and publication of this Report, and its proposals to improve self-regulation, are not designed to regulate or even influence the content of movies, music lyrics or electronic games. The First Amendment generally requires that creative decisions about content be left to artists and their distributors. Rather, the Commission believes the industries can do a better job of helping parents choose appropriate entertainment for their children by providing clear and conspicuous notification of violent content. Industry self-regulation also should support parents' decisions by prohibiting the direct sale and marketing to children of products labeled as inappropriate or warranting parental guidance due to their violent content.

Implementation of the specific suggestions outlined above would significantly improve the present self-regulatory regimes. The Report demonstrates, however, that mere publication of codes is not sufficient. Self-regulatory programs can work only if the concerned industry associations actively monitor compliance and ensure that violations have consequences. The Commission believes that continuous public oversight is also required and that Congress should continue to monitor the progress of self-regulation in this area.

EXAMINING POP CULTURE

Responding to Violence in Popular Entertainment

Parents' Role in Dealing with Television Violence

Dale Kunkel et al.

Dale Kunkel is a professor of communication at the University of California and a senior researcher of the National Television Violence Study (NTVS), a three-year study begun in 1994. Below, Kunkel and seven other researchers who worked on the NTVS give their recommendations to the television industry, policymakers, and parents on how to reduce the potential negative effects of media violence on society. They call on the TV industry to provide less violent programming and to incorporate antiviolence themes into shows, and for policymakers to support further research on the issue. However, they contend that the best way to deal with television violence is for parents to watch television with their children and teach them to critically evaluate its content.

THE RECENT POLITICAL DEBATE SURROUNDING the topic of television violence is quite distinct from controversies of the past. It is clear that the public, most government officials, and many segments of the media industry now accept that television violence contributes to real-world violent behavior, as well as other causes of concern such as increased fear and desensitization. The debate that continues in this realm is not about whether harmful effects of viewing televised violence exist; rather, the controversy has shifted to the question of what

■

to do about the problem. Both means and goals are implicated in the debate. Should violence be reduced, restricted, or labeled, among other options, and if so how and by whom? What is the proper role of government, the media industry, and parents in addressing the issue of television violence?

The findings from the *National Television Violence Study (NTVS)* (1997), along with the extensive body of research evidence upon which the content analysis is based, provide a foundation for some general prescriptions that address the current situation. . . . For the television industry, we call not simply for reductions in violence, but particular sensitivity to avoiding contextual elements that increase the risks of harmful effects. We urge the industry to place greater emphasis on the use of antiviolence themes that may have a prosocial effect when violence is to be included within a program. We also suggest more effective use of program advisories for identifying violent content. These efforts, coupled with continued monitoring by policymakers and more careful supervision of children's viewing by parents, offer realistic potential to reduce the harmful effects of television violence on society. . . .

For the Television Industry

1. Produce more programs that avoid violence; if a program does contain violence, keep the number of violent incidents low.

We do not advocate that all violence be eliminated from television, nor do we profess to know exactly how much is "too much." We trust that interested observers will monitor changes over time in the levels of violence that are measured by this study and will encourage appropriate efforts to limit the presentation of televised violence. Our recommendation is simply to begin efforts to cut back.

This is indeed a long-term goal. The amount of violence on television has been high since its beginnings almost 50 years ago. A substantial reduction in the amount of violence will not happen in one or two years. Tremendous economic risk is inherent in any alteration of established programming patterns that have proven effective in attracting large audiences, which are the television industry's lifeblood. Realistically, such alterations can only be expected to occur slowly.

It will take time for the television industry to accept that the American viewing public will watch and enjoy programming with lower amounts of violence. In the short term, we suggest that producers working in those genres where violence is particularly high (e.g., movies, drama series, and reality-based shows) begin working to bring their levels of violence closer to the industry averages. This, of course, would begin to reduce that industry average, and over time would contribute to lower norms for the overall level of televised violence.

Show the Negative Consequences of Violence

2. Be creative in showing more violent acts being punished; more negative consequences—both short and long term—for violent acts; more alternatives to the use of violence in solving problems; and less justification for violent actions.

This recommendation recognizes that violence is not likely to be declared "off limits." Our focus is on promoting its presentation, when violence is deemed essential, in a manner that should reduce its risk of negative influence on the audience. Much of the portrayal of violence on television is formulaic, a finding that is reflected in the consistency of many of our results on the contextual variables. We encourage producers to move beyond the "old formula" where a bad character stirs things up with repeated acts of violence; where the suffering of victims is seldom shown; and where the bad character continually gets away with the violent action until a good character retaliates with violence of his or her own. All of these factors add to the risk that a given violent portrayal will contribute to antisocial effects on the audience.

3. When violence is presented, consider greater emphasis on a strong antiviolence theme.

There are a number of ways to do this. Among the most obvious are: (1) present alternatives to violent actions throughout the program; (2) show main characters repeatedly discussing the negative consequences of violence; (3) emphasize the physical pain and emotional suffering that results from violence; and (4) show that punishments for violence clearly and consistently outweigh rewards. . . .

4. Make more effective use of program advisories or content codes to identify violent programming.

We recognize that an audience exists for violent programming, and that such shows will always persist to some degree. Nonetheless, many violent programs pose a risk to the audience and that risk should be communicated as clearly as possible, especially to parents. Our data indicate that premium cable channels consistently provide program advisories, but there are many violent programs on other types of channels that are not identified for the audience. When we recommend warnings, we do not mean a simple statement that the program contains violence. Rather, we suggest something more substantial and specific that warns potential viewers about the context of the violence and its corresponding risks, rather than a mere indication of the presence or absence of violence in a program. . . .

For Public Policymakers

1. Recognize that context is an essential aspect of television violence.

Treating all acts of violence as if they are the same disregards a rich body of scientific knowledge about media effects. An appreciation of key contextual factors is crucial for understanding the impact of televised violence on the audience. Furthermore, an appreciation of these elements may contribute to more effective policies should any regulatory action be pursued. At the base of any policy proposal in this realm is the need to define violence and, assuming that not all violence is to be treated equally, to differentiate types of depictions that pose the greatest cause for concern. This requires the careful consideration of the contextual elements we have identified in the *NTVS*. . . .

The bottom line here is that treating all violence the same—as if context did *not* matter—oversimplifies the issue. As public policymakers pursue initiatives to address concern about violent portrayals, it is important that they recognize that context is an essential aspect of television violence.

2. Continue to monitor the nature and extent of violence on television.

Evidence of the harmful effects associated with televised violence is well established and well documented in the complete report of our study (*NTVS* 1997). The stakes are high in terms of the social implications in this realm not so much because of the strength of the effects of viewing violence but more because of the fact that almost everyone watches, most people watch a lot, and most of television contains violence. The effects are pervasive and cumulative. The importance of the issue warrants continued attention to help sensitize the television industry as well as to help alert and inform the public. . . .

For Parents

The ultimate consumers of the information in our report are the nation's television viewers. Of particular interest are parents of young children, who often express helplessness in the face of fifty or more channels of programming across seven days a week. Our study was designed in part to help families make more informed decisions about television violence, and toward this end we have several recommendations for parents.

1. Be aware of the three potential risks associated with viewing television violence.

Evidence of the potential harmful effects associated with viewing violence on television is well established and fully documented in the *NTVS* work. Most attention has been devoted to the impact of television violence on the learning of aggressive attitudes and behaviors. Though not all children will imitate media violence, certain children who are exposed to repeated depictions of a particular nature are at risk for such learning. Arguably more pervasive and often underemphasized are the other two risks associated with television violence: fear and desensitization. A clear understanding of these three effects will help parents better appreciate the role of television in children's socialization.

2. Consider the context of violent depictions in making viewing decisions for children.

Not all violent portrayals are the same. Some depictions pose greater risks for children than do others; some may even be educational and pose very little risk at all. When considering a particular program, think about whether violence is rewarded or punished, whether heroes or role models engage in violence, whether violence appears to be justified or morally sanctioned, whether the serious negative consequences of violence are portrayed, and whether humor is used in a way that trivializes violent behavior.

Different Viewers, Different Risks

3. Consider a child's developmental level when making viewing decisions.

Throughout our work, we underscore the importance of the child's developmental level or cognitive ability in making sense of television. Very young children do not typically distinguish reality from fantasy on television. Thus, for preschoolers and younger elementary school children, animated violence, cartoon violence, and fantasy violence cannot be dismissed or exonerated merely because it is unrealistic. Indeed, many younger children identify strongly with superheroes and fantastic cartoon characters who regularly engage in violence. Furthermore, younger children have difficulty connecting nonadjacent scenes together and drawing causal inferences about the plot. Therefore, punishments, pain cues, or serious consequences of violence that are shown later in a program, well after the violent act occurs, may not be comprehended fully by a young child. For younger viewers, then, it is particularly important that contextual features like punishment and pain be shown *within* the violent scene.

4. Recognize that different program genres and channel types pose different risks for children.

Our findings suggest that children's series may be particularly problematic, especially for younger viewers. Such programming is characterized by unrealistic depictions of harm, frequent use of humor in the context of violence, and little attention to the long-term negative consequences of violence. Although it is tempting for adults to dismiss cartoons as fantasy, these contextual features enhance the risk of imitation of aggression for younger viewers. In addition to genre differences, the type of channel has important ramifications for violence. Premium cable contains more violence than the industry norm, but it also depicts the serious consequences of violence more often. In contrast, public broadcasting contains less violence overall. These differences should be taken into account when planning a family's media environment and viewing habits.

5. Watch television with your child and encourage critical evaluation of the content.

Of all the recommendations we could make, perhaps the most important is to watch television with your child. The only way to ensure that a child appreciates the contextual aspects of violence is to teach a child while viewing. Parents can help a child to understand that violence in the real world may result in more serious injury and may have more long-term repercussions than what is shown on television. Parents also can help children to recognize that nonviolent strategies exist for solving problems in society.

Violent Entertainment and Censorship

Sissela Bok

Sissela Bok is a professor of population and development studies at Harvard University and the author of the 1998 book *Mayhem: Violence as Public Entertainment*, from which this article is excerpted. In it she discusses the emerging debate over whether some types of violent entertainment justify censorship. While government censorship of pornography has long been legally accepted, only since the 1990s have legal scholars begun to debate whether censorship of media violence is similarly justified in order to protect children. Bok summarizes the views of several law professors, judges, and authors who disagree over whether violent entertainment should be protected under the First Amendment right to free speech.

Congress shall make no law respecting an establishment of religion, or prohibiting the free exercise thereof, or abridging the freedom of speech, or of the press, or the right of the people peaceably to assemble, and to petition the government for a redress of grievance.

Amendment 1, Constitution of the United States, 1791

The State shall ensure the accessibility to children of information and material from a diversity of sources, and it shall encourage the mass media to disseminate information which is of social and cultural benefit to the child, and take steps to protect him or her from harmful materials.

United Nations Convention on the Rights of the Child, 1989, Article 17

■

BEFORE THE 1989 UNITED NATIONS CONVENTION on the Rights of the Child (CRC), neither the U.S. Bill of Rights, nor the French Declaration of the Rights of Man, nor any UN convention on human rights had made specific mention of the interests and needs, much less rights, of children. These earlier instruments had been assumed to cover basic children's rights, such as those to life or to freedom from torture, as being no different from the rights of adults. But there had been no provision for interests and rights of children that might be different from those of adults; nor any mention of the special vulnerability of children and of their need for protection from practices such as commercial and sexual exploitation.

The CRC was, likewise, the first international rights document prepared in the age of the new media. The First Amendment's primary focus is on the citizen's freedom to speak out about matters of public concern and in particular to criticize the government, whether by means of the spoken or the written word. The Founding Fathers can hardly be expected to have foreseen the revolution we have now lived through, with respect to the media, from the original focus on the spoken and printed word to all forms of communication still protected as speech. The idea that the state should have any responsibility "to encourage the mass media to disseminate information which is of social and cultural benefit to children and to take steps to protect them from harmful materials" would therefore have struck most authors of earlier documents as beside the point if not preposterous. So would the CRC's claim in article 13 that "the child has the right to . . . obtain information, make ideas or information known, regardless of frontiers."

A New Interest in the Rights of Children

Until the last decade, few legal scholars addressed the problems surrounding contemporary media violence. For many, the main focus remains on the traditional print media and on adult political speech in the United States. While children still rarely figure in most free speech analyses, women now do, especially in feminist debates concerning pornography and censorship. Entertainment violence is taken up primarily, in these contexts, with respect to sexual violence, and children are rarely at issue save as potential victims of sexual abuse. Questions such as whether violence can desensitize children or render some among them more aggressive are seldom discussed in such contexts. By contrast, the risks of exposing young children to pornography on television or the Internet has been extensively debated, most recently in connection with the Communications Decency Act, which was struck down as unconstitutional by the U.S. Supreme Court in June 1997.

The 1990s have at last seen more attention by legal scholars to questions concerning the rights and interests of children in the context of today's media. Newton Minow, former chairman of the Federal Communications Commission, and Craig LaMay, in *Abandoned in the Wasteland: Children, Television, and the First Amendment,* hold that constitutional doctrine recognizes children as a special class of citizens who require special protections and suggest that the Amendment can be used "to serve and protect our children rather than as an excuse to exploit them." The authors make a number of proposals that they claim would interfere in no way with the amendment and that would allow children access to nonexploitative programming: among their suggestions are a ban on commercials during programs for preschool children and fees levied on commercial broadcasters to pay for creating high-quality children's programming.

The Role of the First Amendment

Law professor Cass Sunstein has likewise considered the role the new media play in the lives of children and levels of violence in the programming aimed at them. In *The Partial Constitution,* he argues, as do Minow and LaMay, that the purpose of the First Amendment was to encourage public debate, not to stifle it; and maintains that the Amendment has now come to safeguard speech "that has little or no connection with democratic aspirations and that produces serious social harm." Sunstein holds that regulatory remedies for excessive advertising and exploitative programming on children's television might promote rather than undermine freedom of speech; but that "flexible solutions supplementing market arrangements should be presumed preferable to government command-and-control."

In *Justice and Gender,* law professor Deborah Rhode addresses the debate concerning pornography and violence, suggesting that it ought to be possible to design legislation that would criminalize at least a subcategory of violent material. An example of such legislation "would be criminal prohibitions against sexually explicit visual portrayals of force or violence that lack redeeming literary, artistic, political, or scientific value." Doing so would leave the spoken and the written word uncensored and would not be so phrased as to single out sexual violence against women. In *Speaking of Sex*, Rhode restates her support for such legislation; and even though she acknowledges that it would do little to remedy the prevalence of sexual violence or to promote gender equality, it might "somewhat reduce the availability of targeted material [at] relatively little cost to core First Amendment values. Films like 'Dorothy: Slave to Pain' or 'Pussy on a Stick' are not cornerstones of democratic discourse."

Censorship of Media Violence

Kevin Saunders, in *Violence as Obscenity: Limiting the Media's First Amendment Protection*, agrees with those who would ban visual portrayals of sexually violent material, but he does not see it as constituting the only category that should be banned: "Violence is at least as obscene as sex. If sexual images may go sufficiently beyond community standards for candor and offensiveness, and hence be unprotected, there is no reason why the same should not be true of violence." Saunders highlights what many foreigners view as an odd imbalance in the United States between the regulation of sexual and violent materials; movie ratings, for instance, allow strongly violent films as family fare, so long as they do not contain even mild profanity or sexual content. He examines the scholarly literature and research concerning harm to children and to society from media violence and concludes that some more general form of censorship is needed. Suggesting that the term *obscene* may derive from *ab scaena*, meaning "off stage" Saunders claims that it has often been interpreted as including violence that could not be shown on stage in ancient Greece and elsewhere, adding that obscenity law in the United States was not, until recent decades, limited to sex or excretion.

Saunders proposes that current First Amendment doctrine

should be changed to allow for a degree of censorship of certain expressions of media violence. These expressions should, he suggests, be regarded as unprotected by the First Amendment, just as "sufficiently explicit and offensive sexual material" already is, according to the current test for obscenity, adopted in *Miller v. California*, which asks:

> (a) whether "the average person, applying contemporary community standards" would find that the work, taken as a whole, appeals to the prurient interest; (b) whether the work depicts or describes, in a patently offensive way, sexual conduct specifically defined by the applicable state law; and (c) whether the work, taken as a whole, lacks serious literary, artistic, political, or scientific value.

To the degree that decisions such as *Miller* hold that only the sexual can be obscene, Saunders suggests, "they are simply incorrect and should be disavowed." He considers drafting a new statute, modeled on *Miller*, in which persons can be charged with promoting or intending to promote material that constitutes "violent obscenity," using the *Miller* criteria but reworded so as to specify the appeal to a "morbid or shameful interest in violence" that depicts or describes, in a patently offensive manner, "actual or simulated: murder, manslaughter, rape, mayhem, battery, or an attempt to commit any of the preceding crimes."

Violence as Obscenity

Judge Robert Bork proposes still more far-reaching censorship in *Slouching Towards Gomorrah*. He regards the existing obscenity exception to the First Amendment as unworkably vague and would presumably say the same about Saunders's proposal to treat violent material as constituting an analogous exception. Instead, he argues for shifting back from First Amendment doctrine of the past fifty years to permit straight-out censorship, "starting with the obscene prose and pictures available on the Internet, motion pictures that are mere rhapsodies to violence, and the more degenerate lyrics of rap music." Admitting that it is not clear how effective efforts would be to censor the Internet or digital films viewed at home, Bork claims that lyrics, motion pictures, television, and printed materials are still prime candidates for censorship. He does not discuss counterarguments against censorship, nor specify how his own version would overcome the technical obstacles to enforcing the prohibitions he advocates. Rather, after expressing fear of our coming to be "at the mercy of a combination of technology and perversion," he simply declares: "It's enough to make one a Luddite."

For anyone wishing to counter the societal evils that Bork depicts, the Luddite response of rejecting technological change represents a bitter counsel of despair. It would do little to counter these evils directly and would no more stop the spread of modern media technologies than could the British Luddites who smashed textile machinery in the early 1800s. Ironically, to the extent that modern-day Luddites hope to gain a hearing, their messages will have to travel alongside the welter of images and messages they aim to combat, on the pathways of the very technologies, such as the Internet, that many among them reject.

Protecting the First Amendment

In "Regulating Violence on Television," Judge Harry Edwards and Mitchell Berman are in agreement with Bork on one score: The First Amendment, as presently interpreted, cannot be made to provide the controls on media violence most commonly suggested. But they reach the opposite conclusion to Bork's. The Amendment must be respected, they hold, not reinterpreted, even at stark societal costs. Writing with full and anguished awareness of the impact of media violence in American society, and basing their conclusions on an exhaustive survey of the legal and social science literature, they provide a persuasive analysis of the many different forms of controls of television violence that have been proposed in Congress and elsewhere.

According to Edwards and Berman, television violence is "entitled to the full protection of the rules the Supreme Court has crafted to govern content-based speech restrictions." Try as they might, they do not find that existing social science offers a basis "upon which one may determine with adequate certainty *which* violent programs cause harmful behavior." They argue persuasively that it would not be possible to draw lines with respect to what is and isn't "graphic" or "excessive" violence that would not also exclude many news programs and artistic works that no one would wish to censor. The First Amendment cannot be stretched to tolerate such indeterminate censorship, the authors assert; accordingly they hold that any proposals, such as some of those made by Sunstein, Rhode, Saunders, and Bork, must be rejected to the extent that they involve government regulation of violent programming based on its *content*.

Edwards and Berman conclude that most forms of censorship, whether they involve total banning or require special time zones free from violent materials, cannot be allowed under the First Amendment. At the same time, they argue that measures to label programs as containing violence or not could be lawful if designed to promote parenting; and that the V-chip and other methods to block incoming television programs do not single out particular kinds of content for government-ordained censorship or other control. In other words, parents or other consumers could block whatever type of content they desired, so long as the state did not dictate what form of programming should be prohibited.

A Moral Dilemma

Edwards ends with an eloquent personal postscript reaffirming both his support for free speech and his awareness of the risks that media violence poses for young people and society. He puts the moral dilemma felt by many Americans in personal terms:

> As a constitutional scholar, long-term law teacher, and fervent advocate of the First Amendment, I am not surprised by the conclusions that I have reached. But, as a father and step-father of four children, the husband of a trial judge in Washington, D.C., who works with the perpetrators and victims of juvenile violence every day, and an Afro-American who has watched the younger generation of his race slaughtered by the blight of violence and drugs in the inner-cities of America, I am disappointed that more regulation of violence is not possible. Like many parents of my vintage, I believe, in my gut, that there is no doubt that the trash our children see as "entertainment" adversely affects their future, either because they mimic what they see or become the

potential victims in a society littered with immorality and too much callous disregard for human life. It is no answer for a parent like me to know that I can (and will) regulate the behavior of my children, because I know that there are so many other children in society who do not have the opportunity of the nurturing home that I provide. If I could play God, I would give content to the notion of "gratuitous" violence, and then I would ban it from the earth. I am not God, however, so I do not know how to reach gratuitous violence without doing violence to our Constitution.

We must take seriously the moral tension to which Edwards points, even as we should resist feeling immobilized by conjuring up a rigid dilemma between our duties to safeguard the interests of children and to uphold freedom of speech. Such immobilization is needless on two grounds: first because censorship of the media is less and less feasible; second, because both producers and consumers have many ways to exercise control that are quite unrelated to censorship. The choices confronting consumers, producers, parents, citizens, and societies often clash and are sometimes incompatible in practice. Making one choice may well preclude others. But a strict dilemma between rejecting censorship and safeguarding the interests of children would be one with no escape, no way to transcend or to "go between its horns." As I turn to the efforts made at home and abroad to overcome the broader moral dilemma, Edwards's postscript will stand as a reminder against any inclination to belittle or shunt aside either of its aspects.

The Unappreciated V-Chip

Joanne Cantor

Joanne Cantor is the author of *Mommy, I'm Scared: How TV and Movies Frighten Children and What We Can Do to Protect Them*. In the article below, she discusses the benefits of the v-chip, a tool designed to give parents more control over the types of TV programs their children watch. The v-chip is an electronic device, required in all television sets made after 2000, that allows parents to block out certain shows or entire channels from their TV sets. Cantor believes that the v-chip can be a great aid to parents in limiting their children's exposure to violent entertainment, but that the news media have downplayed both the dangers of TV violence and the importance of the v-chip.

WHEN I WAS GROWING UP IN THE 'FIFTIES, WE were the first family on our block to have a television set. I vividly remember watching the coronation of Queen Elizabeth, with most of the neighbors crowded into our tiny den. What a marvelous convenience! All these free programs came into our homes automatically, and all we had to do was turn on the set to get information and entertainment. We even had the choice between three channels! Before too long, everyone on our block had a TV, and I don't recall any of them questioning whether it was a good idea. Of course, television programming was of a different sort then. For the most part, TV producers behaved as though they were invited guests in America's homes.

■

Reprinted, with permission, from "How to Tame That Trojan House: The Story the Media Won't Tell," by Joanne Cantor, *Television Quarterly*, Winter 2000. Copyright © 2000 by the National Academy of Television Arts and Sciences.

Increasingly Prominent Sex and Violence

Although I've been doing psychological research on the impact of television on children for the past 25 years, we don't need social-science methods to conclude that television has changed and that it is no longer on its good behavior. As the other media have done, television has increasingly used violence and sex to attract audiences, and the most recent trend has been to add explicit gross-out humor to the formula. It's not hard to explain why there are audiences for these themes. Sex and violence automatically attract our attention; our species would hardly have survived if they did not. They also arouse us, prompting an adrenaline rush, and distract us from our mundane problems. And as for gross-out humor, it's no wonder kids are thrilled to hear and see all the words and actions we tell them they must control. Freud was on to something when he said that the essence of humor is the expression of "repressed instincts" camouflaged by "joke-work" to make it acceptable—and the two basic elements he identified were hostility and obscenity (For children, obscenity included what I will politely call "potty issues"). The fact that young males are the most valued by advertisers and the fact that TV producers tend to be young males themselves, probably exaggerates the trend toward these themes.

Producers know easy ways to get our attention, they know sure-fire ways to arouse us and they know how to get a cheap laugh. And sex, violence and crudeness usually translate pretty well to other cultures, making them easily exportable and much more profitable. It doesn't take a lot of creativity or artistic genius to get ratings this way. And now that there are so many channels that have to be programmed, the shortage of creative artists can be met by cranking out movies and TV shows with these themes. I am not saying there are no wonderful programs that probe issues involving sex, violence or even crudeness. But I am saying that there's a lot of stuff that makes money just by parading these elements for their own sake. Clearly, members of the entertainment industry are going to continue making their own choices based on what they think is important (which in many cases is simply making money), and nobody can stop them. That's The American Way.

The Perspective of Parents

But let's look at this situation from the perspective of parents. Here we have a device (more often several of them) that brings some good programming into our homes. Research in fact shows that educational television really makes a difference in children's success later on in life. But if we want that wonderful stuff, all the rest comes into our homes automatically, too. Certainly, if 50's parents had known what television would become, this automatic delivery system would not have been so readily adopted. That wonderful device has become a Trojan Horse, leaving us with no way to stem the tide of violence, sex and profanity into our homes—short of constant vigilance and repeatedly saying "no, you can't watch that."

Parents have very good reasons to want to exercise control. The consensus of rigorous academic research is that repeated exposure to media violence promotes desensitization, encourages aggressive attitudes and behaviors, and often causes repeated nightmares and enduring anxieties. Television news (which increasingly mimics entertainment television) has become a prominent player in these effects as well. But even putting the research aside for a moment, parents ought to have the fundamental right to choose what makes up their home environment. If they want to let in *Sesame Street* and *Blues Clues* while keeping out *Jerry Springer, Howard Stern* and *Sally Jesse Raphael*, they should have that freedom.

The Potentially Revolutionary V-Chip

Here's where the v-chip should come in, but unfortunately, this device has been shunned by the industry. The v-chip is potentially so revolutionary that it should be *a really big, continuing story*. But it's a story that the industry is loath to tell. The v-chip gives parents unprecedented power, power they richly deserve, but they cannot use their power if they don't hear about it. Is it a coincidence that this story is not getting out? I don't think so.

Being the author of *Mommy, I'm Scared*, a book that tells parents to be cautious about their children's television exposure, I know how difficult it is to get TV to help you promote such a message. But even before I was a book author, I came to see how the media felt about parental empowerment when, in May of 1997, I participated in a taping of *The Leeza Show.* The show was set up to invite parents to express their views about the television rating system, which had been introduced in January of that year. What happened at the taping was that parent after parent blasted the new age-based system, saying that it didn't give them the information they needed (did the program have sex, or violence, or what?) and that it enticed their children to watch programs designated for older kids and adults. NBC never permitted that program to air. Not coincidentally, NBC was and still is the only major network to refuse

The V-Chip Is Not Perfect

Since the v-chip was first proposed in 1996, it has been a topic of considerable controversy. While many parents feel it is a useful tool, critics have charged that the ratings system the v-chip relies on is flawed and that the v-chip itself is a first step toward government censorship of violent shows.

As is always the problem with high-minded attempts to protect people from themselves, the people most in need of the protection are those least likely to get it. As Walter Goodman pointed out in *The New York Times* . . ."the ratings will most intensely safeguard children who are already lucky enough to have a set of attentive parents around."

As for the children who are more at risk of infection by television—the ones without two parents at home or with parents who can't figure out the system or are busy making a living or just won't be bothered—they will probably go on spending hours before the tube without knowing they aren't supposed to enjoy dirty words. What effect television may have on a child's behavior and prospects remains uncertain but can it be as great as the effect of having parents who aren't around or don't care?

Parents who do care are those who would presumably

to go along with the subsequent agreement to modify the ratings with content letters.

Few Parents Know the Basics

The result of the media's reluctance to tell the story is that few parents know the basics about the v-chip: That it is available in new TV sets now and that it permits them to block programs automatically based on their ratings. And although many have heard about the TV rating system, practically none of them know that the FV stands for "Fantasy Violence" and the D stands for "Sexual Dialogue and Innuendo."

be vigilant in any case and would probably know without having to be told by abecedarian censors that "Friends" or "Seinfeld" are likely to contain "intensely suggestive dialogue" or that "Homicide" or "Law & Order" may contain "intense violence.". . .

Parenting isn't simple. Neither is labeling television. In our quick-fix culture, the idea of just pressing a button to protect our children is seductive, but it won't work. In fact, the new labels can blur the distinction between high-quality television and programs with gratuitous sex and violence. For example, "The Odyssey," a TV movie based on Homer's epic that was broadcast last May, would have carried a V rating, because it included some violent scenes, even though it was the kind of educational program parents want their children to watch. When the V-chip becomes reality, all shows with a specific rating could be indiscriminately blocked.

Like everyone else, interest groups and politicians have an important right to protest shows they don't like. But they shouldn't decide what people should see. And make no mistake, this new system is the first step by Congress toward suppressing certain kinds of shows.

James Bowman, *New Criterion*, September 1997.

But there are even more important aspects of the story of the v-chip that the media are virtually silent about. One is that some v-chips permit parents to block unrated programs. When the FCC approved the electronic standard for the v-chip, many child advocacy groups urged the Commission to require the device to permit unrated-program blocking. The FCC decided not to mandate this option, but of course, it did not exclude it either. In my book, I encouraged parents to seek out the ability to block unrated programs by buying a new set or a v-chip set-top box, and I suggested they lobby manufacturers to provide this option. I read in the trade papers that the television industry was pressuring manufacturers not to provide unrated-program blocking. But fortunately, some manufacturers listened to parents rather than the television industry, and are giving parents this choice.

Of the few parents who have heard about unrated-program blocking, still fewer are hearing how powerful this choice makes them. First, blocking unrated programs allows parents to protect their young children from the news, which is not rated. By blocking unrated programs, they can prevent their child from stumbling into horrific images of victims of mass shootings or gruesome stories of child molestation and murder. (This seems like a no-brainer to parents, but it is incredibly controversial to almost everyone who works in news.) Second, blocking unrated programs gives the parents of very young children the power to turn normal television reception upside down—they can block everything except programs designated as TV-Y (the most child-friendly rating), something that comes the closest yet to having a childproof cap for their TV. Third, blocking unrated programs allows parents to pressure distributors who are reluctant to rate their programs. Producers are not required to give their programs ratings, but if enough parents block all unrated programs, producers may decide it's a wise business decision to provide this information to parents. This is not censorship, it's capitalism.

And parents have another great tool that they're not hearing about. Many new TVs have the option of blocking entire channels. When I recently discovered that my v-chip was not blocking *South Park*, which according to TV Guide has a TV-MA rating, I simply started blocking the entire Comedy

Channel. This doesn't mean we will never watch that channel. What it means is that my husband and I will select programs on that channel on a case-by-case basis. After all, it's our home and it's our ten-year-old child that we're concerned about.

Parental Control Is Not Censorship

Some members of the entertainment industry call this censorship. But let's be fair: The First Amendment was never intended to force anyone to listen or watch as somebody else exercised their right to free speech. Parents have a fundamental right—indeed a duty—to ensure that the environment in their own home is healthy for their children.

Why is the television industry so uptight about the v-chip and agitated about parents' ability to block unrated programs? Is *NYPD Blue* really dependent on a sizeable audience of child viewers? And does the nightly news really need to target the preschooler demographic? Of course not. What worries the media is that TV's enormous advantage is its automatic entry into homes. So much viewing is unintended—people just drift into watching programs because they're "on." Anything that interferes with this unthinking approach to television exposure may cut into revenues, they fear. This may be true to a certain extent. But it's hard to believe that parents who would block unrated programs during the day would forget that they can unblock them at night when they want to watch news and sports.

Let the Message Out

Parents who want to protect their children from what Hollywood and New York are selling to advertisers are not exercising censorship, but I'll tell you who is: It's the news media who won't provide adequate coverage of the v-chip or TV ratings, and won't give parents the honest story about the risks of exposure to television violence. When I speak to national conferences of parent groups, they are hungry for this information and bewildered by the fact that Jack Valenti, who is paid to support the media's interests, gets more air time than child advocates, mental health professionals and academic researchers. Most parents are shocked to hear that the v-chip is actually available now, and thrilled with the option of blocking unrated programs. And they wonder why they haven't been told before.

So my one request to the industry is, Please! Let the message out. Let parents know about about the risks involved in TV exposure and about the powers they have already won to control the content that enters their homes. You'll still make your profits on programs adults want to see, but parents who care will be given a choice. And maybe our kids will grow up a little bit healthier.

FOR FURTHER RESEARCH

Sissela Bok, *Mayhem: Violence as Public Entertainment*. Reading, MA: Addison-Wesley, 1998.
In her discussion of whether entertainment violence causes real-life violence, Bok begins with a historical examination of the popularity of gladiatorial combat in ancient Rome; moves on to summarize current research on the subject; and concludes with sections on censorship and other approaches to dealing with media violence.

Joanne Cantor, *Mommy, I'm Scared: How TV and Movies Frighten Children and What We Can Do to Protect Them*. New York: Harcourt Brace, 1998.
Cantor presents evidence that media violence harms children and offers guidelines for parents on how to shield their children from violent entertainment.

Carol J. Clover, *Men, Women, and Chain Saws: Gender in the Modern Horror Film*. Princeton, NJ: Princeton University Press, 1992.
Clover challenges the idea that the main appeal of slasher films is for men who enjoy watching women being terrorized; instead, she argues that both men and women become engaged in the plight of the "final girl" who vanquishes the killer at the end of such films.

Denis Duclos, *The Werewolf Complex: America's Fascination with Violence*. New York: Berg, 1998.
French scholar Duclos argues that American society is more obsessed with violent entertainment than other countries are because Americans use crime drama to represent ancient warrior myths.

William Dudley, ed., *Media Violence: Opposing Viewpoints*. San Diego: Greenhaven Press, 1999.
This anthology presents pro/con pairs of essays on the effects of media violence and what should be done about the problem.

Jib Fowles, *The Case for Television Violence*. Thousand Oaks, CA: Sage, 1999.
Fowles argues that the research on television violence is flawed and often contradictory; he believes that, rather than causing aggression, television violence has cathartic effects.

Cynthia A. Freeland, *The Naked and the Undead: Evil and the Appeal of Horror*. Boulder, CO: Westview Press, 2000.

The author explores both classic and modern horror films in an effort to explain why audiences find the fear and disgust that such films provoke ultimately pleasurable.

James William Gibson, *Warrior Dreams: Violence and Manhood in Post-Vietnam America*. New York: Hill and Wang, 1994.

Gibson details how, in the wake of Vietnam, a "war consumer culture" has emerged, with American men eager for war themes in television, movies, video games, and other forms of entertainment.

Jeffrey Goldstein, ed., *Why We Watch: The Attractions of Violent Entertainment*. New York: Oxford University Press, 1998.

The ten essays in this anthology offer various explanations for why audiences are continually drawn to violent film, television, and sports.

Dave Grossman and Gloria Degaetano, *Stop Teaching Our Kids to Kill: A Call to Action Against TV, Movie, and Video Game Violence*. New York: Random House, 1999.

The authors believe that media violence—particularly violent video games, which they call "murder simulators"—makes children more aggressive.

Jake Horsley, *The Blood Poets: A Cinema of Savagery 1958–1999*. Lanham, MD: Scarecrow Press, 1999.

In a series of chronological, film-by-film essays, the author identifies major themes in dark or violent films, covering movies as recent as 1994's *Pulp Fiction* and 1999's *The Matrix*.

Carla Brooks Johnston, *Screened Out: How the Media Control Us and What We Can Do About It*. Armonk, NY: M.E. Sharpe, 2000.

Johnston charges that modern mass media are "killing our culture" and "scaring us to death," in part through constant, graphic portrayals of violence, war, and death.

S. Robert Lichter, Linda S. Lichter, and Stanley Rothman, *Prime Time: How TV Portrays American Culture*. Washington, DC: Regnery, 1994.

Using information from three decades of research, the authors discuss how violence, sex, work, and race are represented on prime-time television.

Michael Medved, *Hollywood vs. America: Popular Culture and the War on Traditional Values*. New York: HarperCollins, 1992.
Film critic Medved denounces depictions of violence, foul language, drug abuse, and sexual promiscuity in popular television, movies, and music.

National Television Violence Study. Thousand Oaks, CA: Sage, 1997.
This is the final report of the comprehensive three-year study begun in 1994 to study the amount of violence on television, the context in which it is presented, and the effects it has on viewers.

Tom O'Brien, *The Screening of America: Movie Values from Rocky to Rain Man*. New York: Continuum, 1990.
The author discusses culturally relevant themes in popular films of the 1980s; his chapter on justice discusses the excessive use of violence in action-revenge films.

Stephen Prince, *Savage Cinema: Sam Peckinpah and the Rise of Ultraviolent Movies*. Austin: University of Texas Press, 1998.
Prince discusses director Sam Peckinpah's efforts to seriously address the issue of violence in his films and how Peckinpah's approach to violence evolved over the course of his career.

————, ed., *Screening Violence*. New Brunswick, NJ: Rutgers University Press, 2000.
This anthology consists of essays that both attack and defend film violence, organized into three sections: "The Historical Context of Ultraviolence," "The Aesthetics of Ultraviolence," and "The Effects of Ultraviolence."

James D. Torr, ed., *Current Controversies: Violence in the Media*. San Diego: Greenhaven Press, 2001.
In this anthology, authors debate how media violence influences children, how serious the problem is, and what should be done about it.

James B. Twitchell, *Preposterous Violence: Fables of Aggression in Modern Culture*. New York: Oxford University Press, 1989.
The author argues that the emergence of violent television shows is only the latest development in a tradition of crass, violent entertainment that he traces back to the early 1700s.

INDEX